LIGHTWEIGHT CLASSIC

*For Liz
Best wishes
[signature]* 1.12.98.

World Masterpiece

World Architecture Building Profile No.1

LIGHTWEIGHT CLASSIC:
Terry Farrell's Covent Garden nursery building

Peter Rice

In Memoriam
PETER RICE

I cannot remember when I first met Peter Rice but it was sometime in 1980 when I had first gone out on my own and I still wanted to keep contact with the work I had done at Farrell/Grimshaw whilst also exploring new fronts. Clifton Nurseries at Covent Garden was a great opportunity to do this. What I did was to take Shelterspan, Peter's invention (with Ian Ritchie), and then to develop a personalised interpretation with Peter. Rather than show possessiveness or react against my assaults on his 'baby' he threw himself fully into this process with a spirit of adventure and curiosity. It was the same later on when I put an even stranger idea to him of putting a tent over the South Bank Arts Centre.

The many lives of the South Bank included what is still my favourite (and first scheme) to tent over the 'rockery' of concrete bunkers, all of which would be kept and treated as objets trouvés. Peter examined my point of view and ideas and came back with an heroic 'beam'. His great beam was all of 200 metres long – and ran high up over the rooftops of all the existing rockery. From it hung tented fabric, balconies, servicing plant and gardens. Perhaps even now it could be built as this scheme seems to have gone full circle.

Peter was great fun to work with, very inventive, full of curiosity about ideas and a great collaborator. I really enjoyed working with him a lot and am very sorry that the chance will never come round again. One of my lasting memories of him was when we both met up sitting in the waiting room of a physiotherapist. By coincidence we had both turned up to see him because of back strain (he and I seemed to indulge in sporting activities well into an age when we should be taking it more easily – he ran a lot and I first hurt my back playing office football!) We sat and doodled and discussed Clifton Nurseries. When I followed him into the physiotherapist the good doctor informed me that he was also a structural engineer and it was an excellent training for a physiotherapist – it is all about mechanics, compression and tension. I remember thinking at the time that this was Peter's great strength, he did not have professional 'barriers', his basic training was an entree to other worlds, including architecture, and his great skill was his ability to see the link between unlikely and disparate parts and then to pursue his convictions with great enthusiasm and creativity, whether conventionally 'normal' or not.

Terry Farrell

First published in 1993 by Cheerman Ltd,
Halpern House, 301 Euston Road, London NW1

ISBN   1-85745 004 3

All rights reserved. No part of this publication may be copied, stored in a retrieval system or transmitted in any form or by any means without the written consent of the publisher and copyright owners.

Introduction © Martin Pawley, 1993

Main text © Paul Jodard, 1993

World Masterpieces is a series title of World Architecture magazine, published by Cheerman Ltd.

Designed by Rob Norridge
Typeset by Wandsworth Typesetting
Printed and bound by Tipogrofia Umbra, Italy

Distributed in the UK and Europe by Lund Humphries Publishers,
Park House, 1, Russell Gardens, London NW11 9NN

Acknowledgements

Martin Pawley invited me to write on the Covent Garden building, and I am grateful to him not only for reminding me of this lost masterpiece but also for his critical eye on the foibles of my earlier drafts. Rob Norridge and Sarah Rayner at World Architecture also contributed much. Terry Farrell opened his archives for the research on this book, and spent much time discussing the building, its design and its context. His colleagues Maggie Jones and Janet Male were equally helpful, and made visits to the Old Aeroworks a welcome pleasure. Brian Forster, Craig Downie, Michael Miller, Philip Tavener, Victor Shanley, Ian Dickinson and Lord Rothschild were all willing to answer my questions, in recalling a project a decade old: I am grateful for their insights – any mistakes are my own.
For supplying photographs and illustrations the author and the publishers are grateful to Farrell & Company, Craig Downie, Knight & Butler, Ove Arup and Clifton Nurseries.   P.J.

World Masterpiece
World Architecture Building Profile No.1

CONTENTS

4	**In Memoriam Peter Rice** – Terry Farrell
9	**Introduction** – Martin Pawley
	The Covent Garden Building – Paul Jodard
17	The Beginnings of a Building
23	Covent Garden Overtures
31	Shaping a Temple to Flora
70	Putting Up a Significant Shed
93	The Drunks and Pigeons Saw to That...

Introduction

A VISIT TO JUDY'S PANTRY

Covent Garden in the early evening of a wet November is not everybody's cup of tea. The fire eaters and acrobats have gone home. On foot you go through cobbled puddles, past the skeletons of market stalls with battered Ford Transits loading up the last unsold goods. The scene is Dickensian. One or two inert figures in anoraks have already taken up their positions under the green-painted archways on the North side of the square. It is almost dark and ground level seems littered with obstacles like hardwood bollards and fence rails. The more progress you make, the sooner you have to turn back and skirt round again.

You always think of Covent Garden as crowded but this evening there are surprisingly few people about. The final approach to the old Clifton Nurseries building, now a diner called Judy's Pantry, is across an open area of cobbles. In the light of the street lamps you can see that the "pocket park" next door to the building is litter-strewn but unoccupied, and the diner itself looks like an Edward Hopper painting. Above its long glazed side wall, feeble bulbs illuminate the first Teflon/coated glass-fibre roof ever used in England.

I make my way towards the front of the building, the

facade with plate glass windows, a full set of columns and a steel framed pediment above. Between the two quaint see-through columns on the right hand side of the facade big green letters stuck diagonally on the glass say "100 per cent beef hamburgers". To the left, where the columns are solid white glass fibre in front of nothing but a painted plywood fence, there is information of a different kind. Black felt-tip messages on the columns read; "Judy you bastard by Naylor... Naylor OK NF. Julie the Slut... Tom Plum Puffter" and so on.

In the gloaming the solid white columns look like giant traffic cones and the skeletal ones look like props from the London Dungeon. Above them are the acrylic capitals, two broken, and above them again, projecting backlit plastic triglyphs along the frieze glow with a final piece of news. Reading from the left they say; "Burgers Cookies

Muffins/J/U/D/Y'S/", then a blank triglyph, then "P/A", then a broken triglyph, and then "T/R/Y/ Ice Cream".

From this distance it is already apparent that the diner is not empty. I can see that there are four people sitting at a table inside. Leaving the "London Dungeon" columns to my left I round the projecting white corner column and open one of the glass doors.

"Yes Sir, what can I do for you sir?" says a smiling man at the counter. Like the pulsating music in the background, this old fashioned courtesy is not out of the modern McDonalds mould. It bespeaks an unusual establishment. Throbbing, but with time to treat its customers as individuals. I scan the illustrated menus overhead and make a hurried decision.

"A... Chickenburger please... And a coke."

"Certainly Sir. If you would like to take a seat someone will bring it to you."

I pay for my food and pass down the narrow passage between the kitchen counter and the jigsaw timber-framed glazed wall, once designed to look like rusticated masonry. To my left the skeleton staff are noisily clearing up as though the diner is about to close, although it seems too early. The clanging accessories of hamburger production are being washed, rinsed, sterilized and stacked. To the right, through the glass panes, I can dimly see the now grimy "Pocket Park" beyond the paved Judy's Pantry terrace, occupied only by stacked chairs with a sign saying "Reserved for Judy's Pantry customers only."

About half way down the long narrow interior of the diner I decide to sit down at a small table for two. Its chairs are of an unexpectedly theatrical design, suitable for dining (below the salt) with Sheriff of Nottingham in Robin Hood's time. The table is different. It is a modern single-legged cantilever job with a heavy base, but you can only see that by lifting the tablecloth. And the tablecloth is not cloth. It looks like chintz but it is plastic. On it is an entry form for a competition that can win you a holiday in the Bahamas. Almost as soon as I have sat down the four other customers leave. The sound of thumping music continues to be punctuated by the clang of putting things away.

For a time I gaze about me like someone who has returned to his native land after a long absence. This was once Clifton Nurseries, filled to the roof with giant ferns, trees and plants. Now its celebrated teflon-coated glassfibre membrane roof is invisible, hidden by a grimy false ceiling out of which shine garish lights. I look carefully. There is only one plant in the whole place, a scrawny survivor on the corner of the counter, tied up to the ceiling with a piece of string to stop it falling down dead.

Few other relics of the building's past survive. The mirrors at the East End, designed to double its apparent length, are still there. But the offices have become lavatories, with paper notices reading "For the use of customers of Judy's Pantry only. Please!". Hanging between their doors and all along the blind partition wall are other evidence of "the culture". There is a cardboard map of Covent Garden. A framed photograph of a pair of legs with a baby looking between them. A picture of a baby seal, and another of two cute mongrel puppies. The music is turned up louder and, as I begin to study every detail of the frieze of red and white tiles above the pinky-brown tiled wall with fanatical intensity, a woman inaudibly deposits an object wrapped in paper and a cardboard cup of coke in front of me.

I unwrap the paper, find out what a chickenburger is, and start to eat it.

"Everything satisfactory sir?" inquires the helpful man after a few minutes. He too has approached unobserved.

I nod, still wrestling with my chickenburger. He waits patiently with an encouraging smile. Eventually I can speak.

"Do you want to close up?"

"No, no, there's plenty of time," he says looking at his

watch. I look at mine too. It indicates half past seven.

"What time do you close," I ask.

"Oh, usually about half past seven. Hardly worth staying open after then. About eight you get the drunks in."

But although I am now alone in the diner he is not trying to speed me on my way. On the contrary he seems to want to chat.

"This is an unusual building," I venture at length.

"You can say that again. You wouldn't believe the people who come here to see it. You can spot them out the front looking at it and taking pictures of it for hours. The carpark people at the Opera have to keep throwing them out from the back because they are not allowed in there. Then they come inside here and ask all sorts of questions. We get Americans, people from Germany, lots from Japan. When they come in they want to look all over the place, upstairs especially. I always help them whenever I can. I mean, I think its an interesting building myself. Never seen another one like it."

"How long has it been... a restaurant?"

"Must be six or seven years now. Ponty's did it first, they got the change. Then we took it. They used to sell plants here before that I believe. What it needs now is closing down for a couple of weeks and a really good clean up."

"Did you ever come here when it was a plant shop?"

"No. I came up from the Anchor and Hope two years ago."

"Do you ever hear any of these visitors talk about the man who designed this building?"

"Yes, they ask about him. Now what's the name? Oh yes. Quin... Quintin Terry isn't it? Something like that."

"It's Terry Farrell actually."

"Terry Farrell eh? I don't remember that name. All I know is that he's supposed to be some sort of an eccentric? That's what I heard."

"Well he's very famous now. You know that huge new building just over Vauxhall Bridge?"

"What that one with, like, green trees?"

I nod again.

"I should have realised. He must have a thing about plants."

In the end I ask him if I can look upstairs too. Again he is most obliging, calling for the keys to the double doors and leading the way up the steep steel steps to the walkway that runs the length of the building. Hanging plants used to be reached from here, but now it is hidden by the false ceiling. From its dizzy height you can see how the false ceiling has been fitted beneath what were once the bottom chords of the steel roof trusses. Up above, and very close in the confined triangular space, the row of huge plywood buttons dimples the Teflon membrane, a stainless steel rigging wire pulling down from the centre of each one.

"They are what holds the roof up," explains the man. "They are alright now we got the pigeon shit out of them."

It appears that, despite the self-cleaning properties of the Teflon coating, vast accumulations of guano in the dimples have from time to time disfigured the membrane when seen from the "Pocket Park" side. But now they have got rid of the pigeons and there is no longer a problem.

By the time we return to the ground floor, the staff are carrying in the outside chairs and switching off lights. Thanking the man for his kindness I take my leave and, moving discreetly out of sight, watch them finish the process of closing up and going home. For several minutes I stand and watch the building in the light of the street lamps refracted by a thin drizzle, then I too turn and make my way past the obstacles back to the underground station.

The Covent Garden Clifton Nurseries building has fascinated me ever since I first went inside it at the Press opening in December 1981. I think the reason is that, just as some human beings achieve greatness in proportion to the astonishing number of contradictions they can embody, so can a

piece of architecture attain greatness in the same way. And in this building is a bundle of contradictions without parallel. At the lowest level it is a temporary building on a glamorous site that is already five years past its sell by date. Beyond that it is a cheap building that was designed for a wealthy and fastidious client. Then it is a Classical design drawn up by an architect who knew (at that time) nothing about classicism, and a building erected in a place where not only does every vista end in a Classical facade, but in the Classical facades of historically important buildings. Beyond that it is a design in the shape of a Tuscan Temple that was erected where there is really only room for half of one. Furthermore it is a Tuscan Temple made out of steel, glass and teflon coated glassfibre fixed in place with technology borrowed from racing yachts: a step toward the concept of a high-tech Classicism that has been talked about by architects for a decade, but so far only really been exploited by this one architect in this one building. Terry Farrell has no difficulty coming to terms with the axial planning principles of ancient Rome while masking a carpark. He can achieve the effect of Doric colonnade and entablature by means of ticky-tacky, glassfibre, skeletal steel bars, acrylic capitals and a frieze of living plants. He is the only architect who could ever have conceived of it.

From the beginning this little building with its jumble of elements was touched by a kind of omnivorous, untrammelled genius. Everything about it, from its client's original idea, to its architect's wild and ingenious design, to its innovative light-structures engineering by the late Peter Rice, to its first tenant's verdant display of energy and enterprise, all of it was pure magic. And when you analyse that magic, most of it consists in making something out of nothing, which was the once and future genius of Terry Farrell – as visible in the conception of the giant Alban Gate, built in thin air over London Wall, as it was 10 years earlier on that tiny site in Covent Garden. Notwithstanding such spectacular later commissions, and

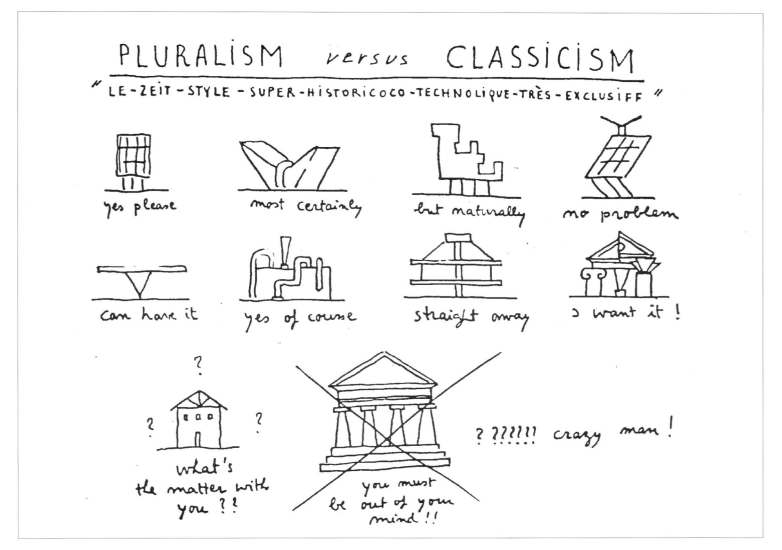

perverse as it may sound, Clifton Nurseries Covent Garden will be remembered long after it is demolished. In 1981, with some trepidation, I dubbed it "The Barcelona Pavilion of post-Modernism". Today I would not even be surprised if, like that illustrious predecessor, it did not go down once only to rise again in replica.

Who would do such a thing? There is already intriguing evidence of another mind into which its image has penetrated. On page 56 of the catalogue to the current Prince of Wale's Vision of Europe exhibition there is a cartoon by Leon Krier entitle "Pluralism versus Classicism". In it he has drawn a number of bizarre buildings with enthusiastic captions underneath them; "yes please!", "No problem", "straight away" and so on. The only rejected building is a serious representation of a Greek Temple, which draws the caption; "You must be out of your mind!!" All very predictable of course, and indeed only an updated variant of an earlier Krier cartoon published 10 years ago. But between 1983 and 1992 a difference had crept in. This time around, above the caption "I want it", the sketch has been changed. Now it shows something that bears so much more than a passing resemblance to Clifton Nurseries that it surely can be nothing less than an act of homage.

I commend Paul Jodard's account of the making of a minor masterpiece.

Martin Pawley
December 1992

THE BEGINNINGS OF A BUILDING

Terry Farrell's garden shop for Clifton Nurseries in Covent Garden, London, happened at a key moment in his career. The building served as a springboard for his later work, not only because of its prominent position, but also because of the opportunity his client, Jacob Rothschild, offered him. Farrell observes today that he has often been fortunate, lucky even, in getting commissions for interesting sites - "I never got offered office buildings in the back streets of provincial towns."

Terry Farrell was born in 1938. He had always been interested in art and painting, and decided to study architecture, at King's College Durham, the then architectural school for Newcastle University. After a year in London working for the London County Council and later for Stillman and Eastwick Field, he won a Harkness Fellowship to study in the United States of America, under Louis Kahn, Denise Scott Brown and Robert Venturi, worked in New Jersey and spent time in Japan, thanks to an RIBA travel grant. Returning to London in 1964, he worked with Colin Buchanan before setting up in partnership in 1965 with Architectural Association graduate Nick Grimshaw, whom he had met during his earlier period in London.

It was a commission to rehabilitate student housing for the Church Commissioners that made a name for the practice as high-tech specialists. As Farrell recalls, under the 1970s Labour Government there were plenty of

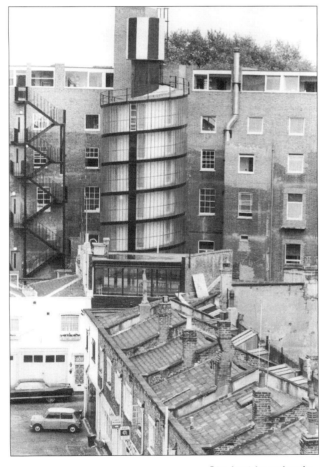

Student housing in Paddington, designed by the Farrell Grimshaw partnership

In this housing for the Maunsell Housing Association Farrell used a modular system in which the same timber frame could be used on different sites, while still providing variety in external appearance.

incentives to build industrial parks on the outskirts of towns, as industry was seen a means of economic recovery, and plenty for new residential building through Housing Associations. But if new architects wanted work, they had to go and find it. Nick Grimshaw's crisp style with new materials - demonstrated in the glass fibre bathroom pods of the practice's best-known student housing project in Paddington - made him the right partner to deal with the industrial work, while Farrell found that the best way to find a Housing Association client was to become one yourself (an opportunity later denied by legislation, which put Government approved housing managers in charge, though as Farrell points out ruefully one of the managers he was obliged to hand over to was later jailed for theft of Association funds.)

Two of the Farrell and Grimshaw housing schemes, one for Maunsell Housing Association, the other for Warrington New Town, were important in developing Farrell's personal approach to urban context and to the use of industrial elements. Not in terms of cladding, or what Farrell describes as "TV window architecture, all rounded corners and blank centres", but in the sense of creating opportunities for flexibility and customization in the simple context of timber-framed housing. The two schemes, in their different ways, tried to allow for the final owners to adapt their homes to their own life-styles by exploiting or adding-on individual elements. For example, Farrell's diaries from 1979 to 1981, when the Oakwood scheme at Warrington was nearing completion, frequently refer to his search for a sponsor to make the "add-on" system more widely available.

Although the Farrell Grimshaw partnership did not formally dissolve until 1980, in a sense Farrell's separate career began at the Architectural Association in 1975. The invitation to him speak there had come from Charles Jencks, who by his own account had been interested in Farrell since an RIBA lecture Farrell and Grimshaw had

At Warrington Farrell looked at a different problem: using a modular system that would allow for efficient building while also encouraging tenant to develop and customise their homes themselves, either by extending or personalising the accommodation from a kit of parts devised by the architect.

A physical articulation of the language of post-Modernism - the staircase in Charles Jencks' London house, designed by Farrell with Jencks and Maggie Keswick.

given five years before. Charles Jencks is an American critic and writer on architecture, living in London, and at the time he was the leading proponent of American post-Modernism in the UK. He was planning, with his wife, the writer Maggie Keswick, to transform their house in London into a major architectural statement, and he turned to Terry Farrell for help with the development and expression of this plan. He needed "the resources of an office and of a flexible, experienced architect to help work it through and build it".

There is no doubt that the Jencks house came at a turning point in Farrell's career. "I started work on the Jencks house", he remembers, " to help with the spatial exercise, organizing the rooms around the main staircase, and making the staircase an internal feature. I'd been working on similar problems in space planning and land use already: I knew the spatial language, and that was what I brought to the building. The decorative language, the terms of post-Modernism, was not why I was there."

Farrell worked particularly on the central staircase and the upstairs study, but all involved agree that the initial planning process for the house was based on joint decisions between Maggie Keswick, Charles Jencks and Terry Farrell. Because the discussions between them were not merely practical, but concerned the ideas and principles of the new architectural credo, post-Modernism, that were to be physically embodied into the house, they served also to help release the creative energy that Farrell had been building up but holding back. Despite some disagreements with Charles Jencks about decoration, Farrell and he remain good friends. "Charles was very eager and ambitious for the house", Farrell recalls, "and once the building work was well ahead and the decorative work started, his own ideas came more to the fore. I didn't always agree with these, but as he was the client and was on site all the time, there was little I could do. It's often a problem, and one of the reasons I've never been excited

The Colonnades housing scheme at Paddington.

about doing a lot of private housing."

More important than the theoretical consequence of working with Charles Jencks was the fact that Maggie Keswick, introduced Farrell to Jacob Rothschild (now Lord Rothschild). Jacob Rothschild had decided to develop his own interests independently of the family business: he had, for example, taken a stake in Colnaghi's, an established firm of picture dealers in Bond Street in London. More significantly for Farrell, he had also bought into Clifton Nurseries, a nursery and garden shop in St John's Wood, with the aim of developing a series of nurseries across London and the Home Counties. Rothschild's idea was that unused urban sites - especially those temporarily vacant and awaiting redevelopment - could be turned into "pocket parks" on the New York model, with accompanying garden centres or shops. This would make a better social contribution than the dreary alternative of car parking, and would be feasible on a short-term basis provided temporary, low-cost buildings could be found. It was for this project that he needed a special kind of architect. As Lord Rothschild recalls, "Charles Jencks had talked to me about the work of Terry Farrell, which I liked very much."

By 1979, Jacob Rothschild had already written to the central London boroughs enquiring about possible sites, and one reply, from Westminster City Council, had mentioned that a site on the Colonnades development in Bayswater was available. Here was co-incidence twice over, for Terry Farrell had been responsible for the housing development at the Colonnades between 1974 and 1976, when 240 units were built around a group of retained Victorian houses. Part of the scheme had included a proposed new municipal library, which Nicholas Grimshaw was to design, but cuts in local government funds and delays in the design process meant it remained unbuilt. Ironically, one of Farrell's first independent buildings was now to be constructed on a site for which under the Farrell/Grimshaw practice his former partner had been making designs.

COVENT GARDEN OVERTURES

By 1979 the refurbishment and conversion of the former fruit and vegetable market in Covent Garden was well in hand. The redevelopment plan had caused a major confrontation between the local residents and the developers, a confrontation to which the highly visible, metropolitan aspect of the area, and its rich architectural heritage, contributed much. One of the main concerns of the various resident's associations and groupings was to secure community facilities, in particular public open space and gardens. One of their most precious areas "saved from the developers" was the Italian Garden in the north-east corner of the Piazza. Money had been raised from the local community and local businesses, together with a grant from the Manpower Services Commission, to convert waste ground into this garden area, with trees and planted areas in troughs. The lease on this parcel of land, owned by the Royal Opera House, was up for renewal at the end of 1979. There had been problems with the maintenance of the garden on a regular basis, partly because of funding and partly for organizational reasons. At the same time the Royal Opera House was developing its own plans for future expansion.

The rebuilding of the market buildings in the centre of Covent Garden had also encouraged developments in

Two views of the Covent Garden Piazza prior to the redevelopment of the Italian Garden site.

The Italian Garden: overgrown and neglected despite the good intentions of the community.

the surrounding area: Terry Farrell was already working on plans for the Comyn Ching site, to the north-west of the Piazza, and on a building in nearby Earlham Street for Christina Smith, owner of Smith's Galleries. Christina Smith was a member of the Covent Garden Forum, which, like the Covent Garden Residents Association, was monitoring the development of the area. A third such body, with representatives on it from the other two, was the Covent Garden Open Spaces Committee. This body looked after the Italian Garden, and Christina Smith was a member - she had also sponsored one of the trees in the Italian Garden. One of her other concerns was with the churchyard of St Paul's Church, then used for car-parking, to generate much-needed revenue for the church. Christina Smith felt it too could become a public space, or a public garden, if the revenue could come from elsewhere. Thus the idea came up of putting a garden centre in the churchyard. Terry Farrell drew up proposals for a pavilion on the site, and for furniture for a children's play area, but the idea of a garden centre in a churchyard seemed too obtrusive. However, a garden centre attached to the Italian Garden was a different proposition, and in August 1979 Terry Farrell took Jacob Rothschild to meet Christina Smith.

After informal meetings with representatives of the Covent Garden Forum, and discussions with Clifton Nurseries, Terry Farrell produced in November 1979 a "general proposal for a small garden centre and re-design of the Italian Garden site" for the Forum's comments. The sketches and plan show a building with three elements, an entrance backing on to Maxwell's wall - the back wall of no 17 Russell Street - a garden shop on the King Street site and an arcade linking the two. The entrance would terminate in a pavilion which would echo the pavilion in St Paul's Churchyard, and the garden would be a sunken one. There are a number of variations to this plan, with different entrances proposed, such as a

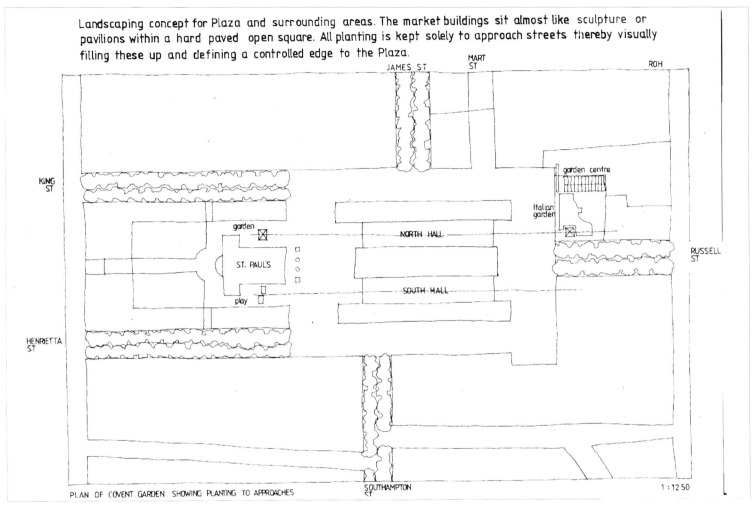

Farrell's first idea was to restore the original symmetry of the Piazza by linking garden and play areas in St. Paul's churchyard to the Italian Garden site.

Victorian conservatory or a classical arch, but the underlying plan provided offices and storage space for community associations, and a children's play area, another feature important to the residents. As to the off-centre King Street axis, the first design interestingly shows a screen motif that extends beyond the area of the garden to sit square on the axis.

After discussions with the Opera House Development Sub-Committee in January, Farrell put in a preliminary planning application in March 1980 for the L-shaped building. However, this proposal was seen by the Forum too encroaching, both spatially and commercially, and more modest plans were put to a meeting with the local community and the Royal Opera House in early March 1980. This meeting perhaps brought to a head the

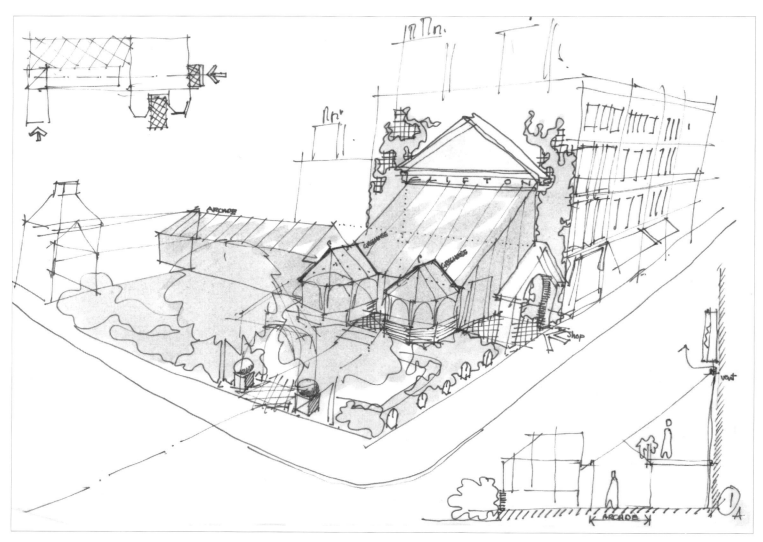

One of the early proposals for the garden had these Victorian conservatories fronting an arcade running along the side wall.

residents' feeling that they were being manoeuvred out of yet another public space by unsympathetic business interests, on the one hand, and on the other the Opera House's concern that the garden was being neglected. There was much talk about "wine-bar types" taking over the garden, for example, and restricting access to *bona fide* residents. As the architect Jim Monahan, who for many years has been involved in planning and politics in Covent Garden, puts it, "there wasn't much opposition to the building or its design. It was more what the building seemed to represent that upset people."

A compromise was suggested, in which Clifton Nurseries would take 20 percent of the site for a garden shop, as well as redesigning and replanting the Italian

Garden, but even this, in the atmosphere of the meeting, was not well received. After the meeting Terry wrote to Jacob Rothschild "I strongly believe that the meeting need not be the end of the affair… The resident's use of this garden with Clifton's occupying 18% is a very workable partnership." A longer letter followed on March 14th. This reiterated the argument that, if the residents have not done well with one hundred percent of the space, concentrating their efforts, with Clifton's support, on eighty percent might improve the garden. Farrell also stressed that Clifton's proposal should not be seen as "purely commercial… Your interests are much broader and more civic in ambition."

After further discussions, including conversations

An alternative scheme had less imposing front entrance, but both of these earlier schemes were considered too commercial an intervention.

BY HAND

14 March 1980

Jacob Rothschild Esq
Rothschild & Sons
New Court
St Swithins Lane
LONDON E C 4

Dear Jacob

re: COVENT GARDEN

Since speaking to you yesterday I have received the Minutes of our meeting with the residents and ROH. The only argument against Cliftons' proposals is that without 100% of the Italian Garden space, the residents cannot do what they want. The arguments against the residents are:

1) they havn't performed well on maintaining this space when they had 100% and therefore for them to have 80% would give them a more realistic and manageable bit of land to maintain.

2) with Cliftons' backing in money, materials, advice and support the public and ROH would be further reassured that the residents' 80% will be well maintained.

3) the residents, even if they had 100% and then performed well on it, would still not answer the need of the community at large for a civic/architectural solution for a site which has wider importance to the public than just serving the local residents' needs; this argument will increase in importance once the market buildings are open, and the whole of the marvellous reconstruction is opened to the world.

4) Cliftons are not coming in as a normal "commercial" concern. They are offering <u>partnership</u> and are not looking for a big profit. Frankly, Jacob, if it was known publicly that the lion's share of the profit was going to support the community space, the residents' case for 100% of the land would not get much sympathy. At present, Cliftons are labelled as just another commercial interest not only by the residents but to some extent by the Opera House and yet I believe your interests are much broader and more civic in ambition. In addition, I would myself believe that Cliftons could turn all profit (providing costs are amply covered) to the residents' land and still benefit enormously in the long run from the significance of location and the future potential, once renewed leases are sought.

/ continued ......

- 2 -

Jacob Rothschild
14 March 1980

5) Delaying matters a year to give the residents a chance on 100% of the land is not a satisfactory answer as with a very short time after this year's lease commences, the market buildings will be complete. The contrast between these buildings and the Jubilee site with the Opera House gap will therefore ve very evident for many months before a chance arises for the lease to be reconsidered - and as we all know possession is 9/10ths of the matter and it could be more difficult to gain your 20% in a year's time than now.

I gather the Opera House Board Meeting is on 25 March. If you feel you need anything further from me before then to help anyone supporting our case on the Board, please do not hesitate to let me know.

Yours sincerely

Terry Farrell

This letter from Farrell to Rothschild sets out some of the arguments in favour of Clifton Nurseries taking over the site: "I believe your interests are much broader and more civic in ambition", he writes.

between Jacob Rothschild and Sir John Tooley at the Royal Opera House, the Italian Garden was reprieved for a further six months, rather than the year hoped for by its defenders, while Clifton Nurseries put in a revised planning application for the site. This Farrell did in May 1980, and the Covent Garden Open Spaces Committee lodged an objection to the application at the beginning of July. This highlighted the facts that open space would be lost, that the Italian Garden had been built with public money, and that the application did not conform to the general plan for the area, the Covent Garden Action Plan (a Freudian slip in the Committee's letter described this as the Action Ban). Nonetheless the Greater London Council approved the proposal.

A further meeting between Clifton Nurseries and the Royal Opera House was planned for 26th September, in order to start negotiations for a lease. In August Jacob Rothschild wrote to Farrell suggesting the Opera House might give up part of their car park to leave the original size of the Garden intact, and, preparing for the meeting, he asked: "did you decide to make a model?" Farrell cheekily added to the letter "Did he decide to pay for it?" The model was indeed made for the meeting, and paid for by Jacob Rothschild. The Royal Opera House agreed to grant Clifton Nurseries a lease on the garden, on condition that the building did not occupy more than eighteen percent of the site, and that the rest was laid out as a garden and maintained for the public.

The garden was designed by Victor Shanley of Clifton Nurseries, who was also responsible for building it. The basic plan was for brick embankments on the sides of the garden open to the Piazza, with seating set into the walls, and planting behind leading to a central paved area. This was in the form of a square, crossed by a diagonal path leading from the Russell Street corner of the site, and into the Piazza past the entrance to the shop. The edges of the square were marked by a line of white

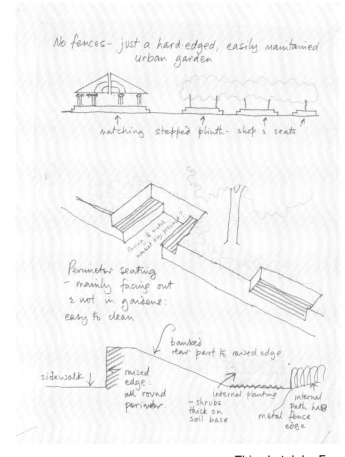

This sketch by Farrell for seating options for the Jubilee Garden show him linking the garden shop with the garden and the site with the Piazza as a whole.

brick, and the rest paved with York Tone slabs. Against the back wall of the garden a trellis was erected, to provide depth and to conceal the view of the wall and the carpark beside it. The garden was designed as an urban one, and so easy to maintain; the main planting areas were in the front corner, where Russell Street entered the Piazza, and against the back wall. Victor Shanley looked for "a general effect of greenery, rather than patterns of flowers: after all, this wasn't some municipal park." He recalls: "I was particularly concerned about the seating, not just the choice of benches to put around the central square, but also the seating let into the walls. My first choice was for a slotted aluminium seat, which would have gone well with the technology of the building, but in the end plainer concrete benches were used."

The garden was not the only amenity planned for the site: the lighting designer David Hersey, who at the time was lighting the new musical *CATS*, was involved in discussions for a permanent light-show to be projected onto the back wall over the trellis. While this came to naught, an alternative idea of a specially painted mural for the wall did not. This mural was commissioned and paid for by Jacob Rothschild. Other plans had included a children's play area, a fountain and a sculpture park: indeed one exhibition of sculpture was held in the garden shortly after the building opened.

Farrell not directly responsible for the garden: as he now points out "it was Clifton's part of the project." In fact, Farrell and his colleagues were already involved not only in planning and construction details, but also in conceiving the shop interior and fittings. As early as a client meeting in April 1981, for example, the question of what stock the shop would carry was already on the agenda, as was the way in which the shop would relate to the surrounding garden: "clients want unusual garden related to external area" reads one handwritten note on the meeting, ending "future supervisor is very image conscious."

SHAPING A TEMPLE TO FLORA

The garden building at the Colonnades was intended to be a model for future sites, but the challenge of Covent Garden required a new idea.

The design history of the Garden Shop at Covent Garden needs to be understood within the context of Farrell's general brief from Jacob Rothschild and Clifton Nurseries. As we have seen, Rothschild's plan was to develop a chain of garden shops, which would be intentionally temporary structures on unused urban land. In stating that he may have had in mind the example of the great gardener/architect, Joseph Paxton, whose Crystal Palace also borrowed garden technology for a temporary and very visible site. Update and dramatically downsize Paxton's idea, and switch glass and cast iron to steel and plastics, and you do indeed find the same concept of standard parts and regular elements, disposed in a novel fashion, that underlay the first Clifton Nurseries building in Bayswater. Of the wider ambitions of Covent Garden, Lord Rothschild says "I liked the idea of doing something playful on a temporary site like the one in Covent Garden and felt that Terry Farrell's imagination would be particularly appropriate."

Be that as it may, Farrell's original plan was to produce a building module that could be adapted and customized to each site, and the early plans for developing Rothschild's concept included at least two further sites in

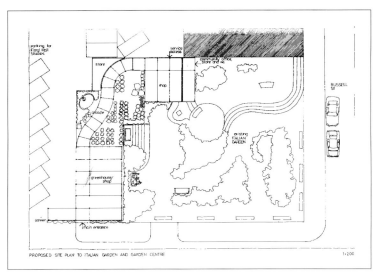

This proposed plan for the site was intended to leave as much of the garden intact as possible: its discretion is perhaps its weakness.

the Home Counties, while other sites in Central London were proposed to Farrell, but apparently not studied.

The first proposal for the Colonnades garden centre was for a standard greenhouse unit with add-ons, similar to work Farrell had done on an earlier industrial site in Bedfordshire, and harking back as a concept to his housing association work of the mid-1970s. After meetings with Clifton Nurseries management, this pre-fab idea was discarded in favour of a purpose-built modular unit, still based on standard tubular steel parts, and incorporating high-tech cladding, which could provide the variation in interior spaces and internal thermal control that a standard greenhouse could not. According to Farrell, this new unit was intended to be used, modified as to the particular site requirements, as the centre building in all future garden developments. At the Colonnades, this is what happened, but in the case of Covent Garden, this intention could not be fulfilled.

As we have seen, the political history of the site restricted the building to a strip on the edge of the garden site, and so a centrally-placed flowing greenhouse as at the Colonnades was no longer an option. The notion of a middle unit with added features was however retained in the first proposal, drawn up in the scheme shown to the Covent Garden Forum in September, 1979. This had the central shop unit lying across a swathe of the site, with a grand entrance backing on to Maxwell's wall on the south side, and a lesser entrance in the opposite corner. The proposal was unacceptable to the Forum as too encroaching and too commercial, and in any case, when costed it proved too expensive for a temporary development. For at that time the Royal Opera House intended to redevelop the land for a second auditorium within five years. Despite these setbacks, Farrell applied for planning permission for this L-shaped building in February 1980, realising that the impasse over the Italian Garden would have to be solved in time, probably on the basis of the garden

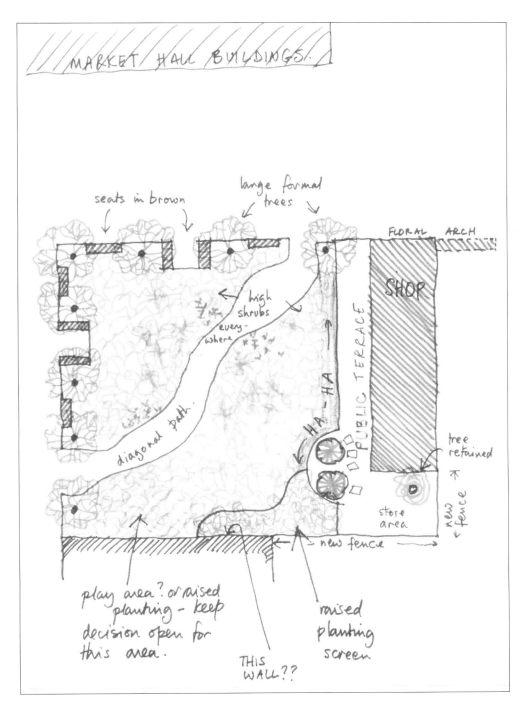

Once it was clear that only twenty percent of the site would be available to build on, Farrell developed the plan of a building down the left-hand strip of the site, with a public sales terrace opening onto the garden. The responsibilities for the different zones were set out in the block plan (below).

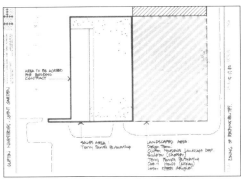

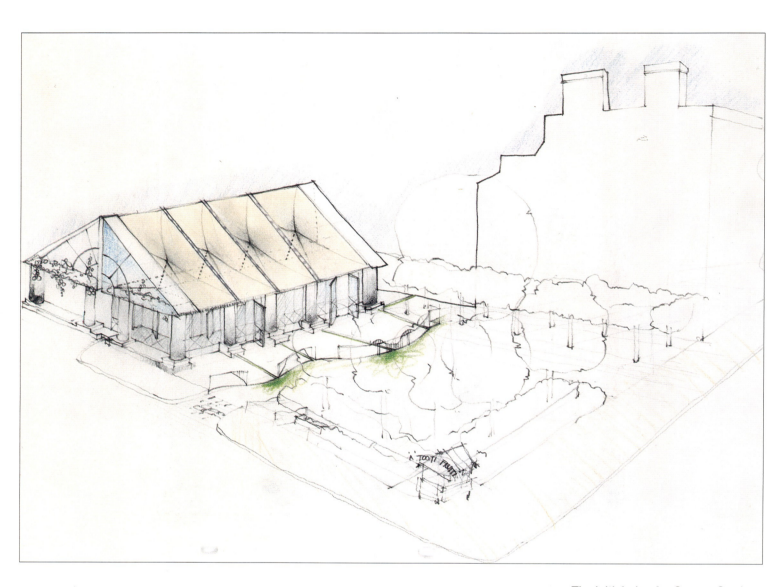

The initial plan for Covent Garden was to link the Italian Garden site (left) with the perspective down King Street (facing, below). A design based on a temple, as in this early sketch (above) would re-integrate St Paul's Church into the piazza and close the axis down King Street (facing, above: the church is highlighted in red.)

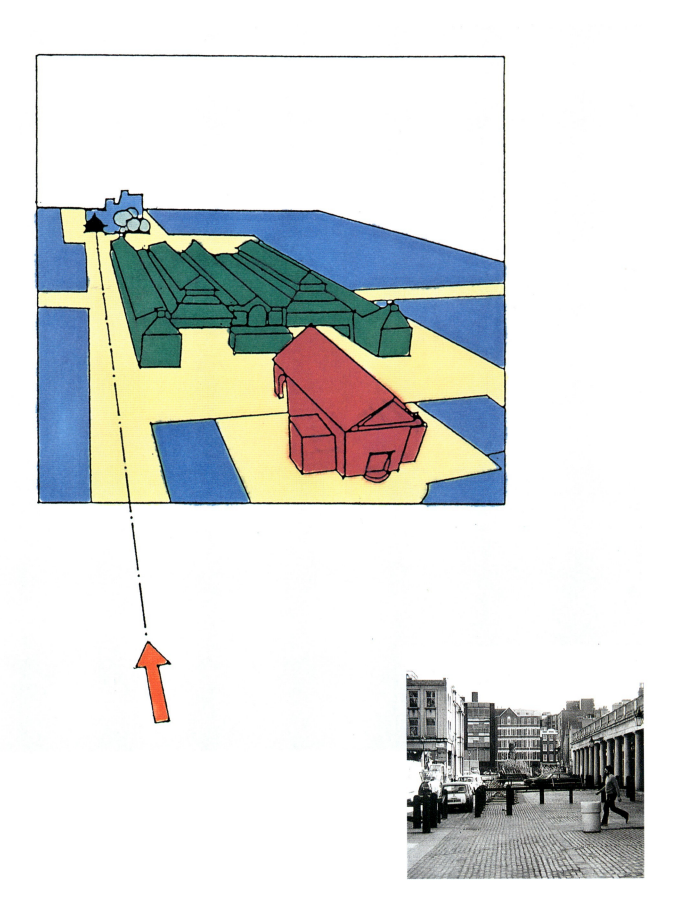

This letter of November 27th sets out Farrell's final approach. Accepting the neeed for a narrow building crowded to one side, he insists it be visually strong, to deal with the contextual considerations of the site. He also draws Jacob Rothschild's attention to "a kind of classical revivalism called Post-Modernism... all the rage with students now."

27th November 1980

The Hon Jacob Rothschild
P D Colnaghe & Co Ltd
14 Old Bond Street
London W1

Dear Jacob

I spoke to Phillip last night about the Italian garden site. I would recommend you now proceeded as follows :

1. Build only along one side of the open site i.e. along the complete length of the north fence adjoining the carpark. The amount of open space for sales you then take is up to you and the Open Spaces Committee.

2. Just build a simple lean-to off the peg greenhouse with minor modifications to make it more elegant. I gave Phillip last night some photographs of an off the peg conservatory we have just built which provides workers amenity space at a factory. We modified the gable ends to make them more attractive, otherwise it is a standard thing, ordered, designed, manufactured and erected in about 6 weeks for about £15,000 (excluding foundations) and it is as big as the Colonnades greenhouse.

3. Architecturally put all your eggs in one basket, i.e. an arch or screen on the west face closing the long vista down King Street. Planners, Opera House (Dartington) and most of those involved seem to agree that this is where the impact should be. Unlike the Colonnades which is an open nondescript site, this one is viewed from limited angles and <u>contextural</u> considerations dominate the architectural requirements. I am convinced this is the solution and that it will get support. As for cost, we are doing and have done several projects with architectural students where we lead the design and they build (e.g. in Warrington New Town **they are making entry** front doors and porches of a 150 house estate different one from another). We work initially with the teaching staff and then use their excellent in-house workshops to prefabricate the components ready for quick site assembly. Only the materials have to be paid for. Here in London I know the heads of teaching staff of all the central schools and feel I could get something up - particularly as a kind of classical revivalism called Post-Modernism is <u>all the rage</u> with students now. I enclose the latest issue of Architectural Design (edited by Charles Jencks) with examples of classical post-modernism indicated.

Yours sincerely

Terry Farrell

shop only taking a part of the space. Outline planning permission was granted in July 1980, though the letter of confirmation was not sent out until November.

This planning consent, and a further round of meetings between the Opera House, Clifton Nurseries and the Forum, led to the key design formulation, sketched out in a note accompanying a letter to Jacob Rothschild on the 27th of November 1980. This incorporated for the first time the idea of a fully pedimented facade fronting a long, narrow building half the width of the pediment. The idea of a half-used facade was a very neat solution to the two problems facing the architect. On the one hand the building was only allowed to occupy a narrow strip of the site - there were even arguments later about

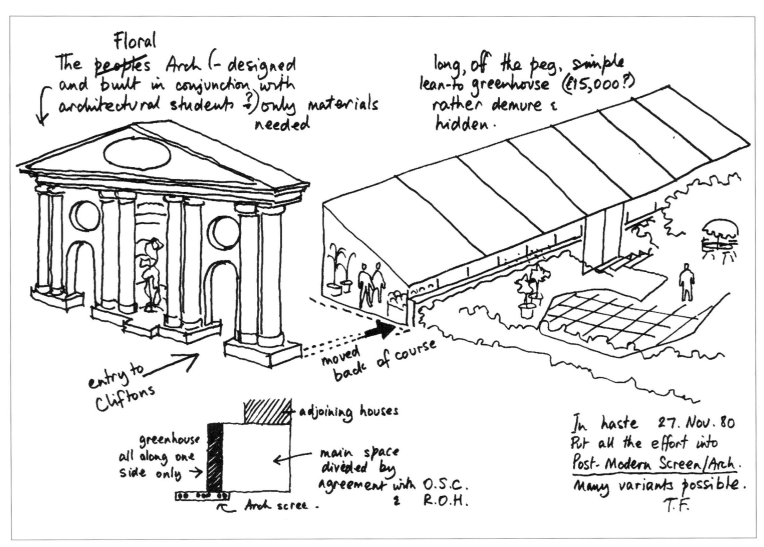

This drawing accompanied the 27th November letter. It shows the idea of a trompe-l'oeil arch for the first time, framing a "rather demure and hidden" greenhouse. To be designed and built by architectural students, only materials will be needed for a peoples arch - corrected to floral arch.

Two views of Covent Garden during redevelopment

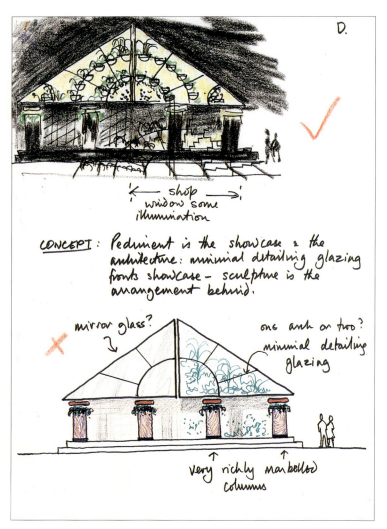
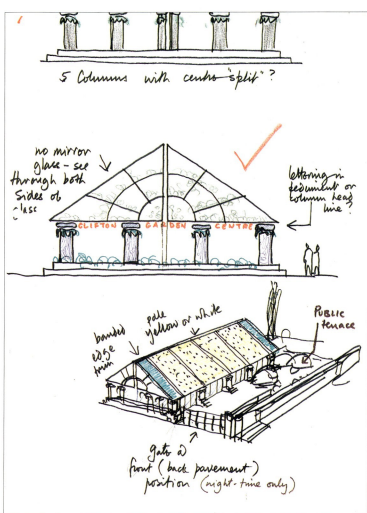
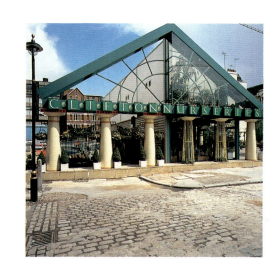

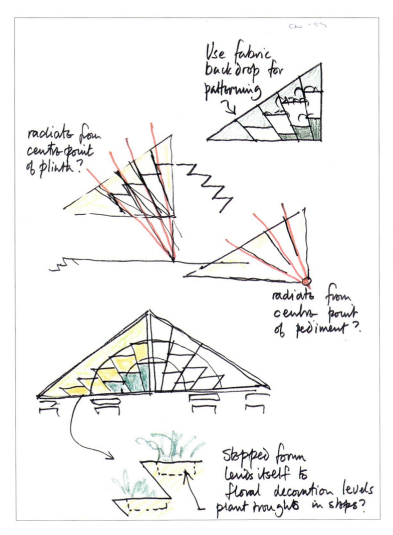
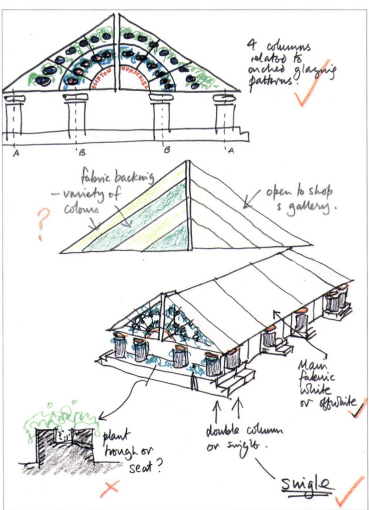

These four sketches show different arrangements of the pediment and colonnade fronting the building: with split columns and single columns, with a ziggurat in the pediment or a triangular pattern, mirror glass or planting troughs on the blank side. Some solutions are ticked as approved, others carry notes and question marks. The final design (facing, below) shows how the design evolved still further in the completed building.

This sketch by Farrell shows Shelterspan involved in the garden shop for the first time. As well as the roof, Shelterspan, headed by Peter Rice, would also be asked about a "crinkly tin" wall on the back of the building.

whether the 18% finally agreed upon included the paving stones around the building or not. But on the other hand the edge of the site sat squarely on the axis of the vista down King Street, and clearly, any satisfactory architectural solution needed to respond to this axis with a strong enough statement for the area as a whole, as well as specifically balancing the facade of the London Transport Museum on the opposite side of the Piazza. The theatrical, *trompe-l'oeil* device of the pediment did require the Opera House to lease a narrow strip of land adjacent to the site, but since it would obscure the inelegant view of their car park, about which they were concerned, their support could be expected.

The letter of 27th November accompanying the first sketch (illustrated on previous page) ends, some might say prophetically, with Farrell sending Jacob Rothschild a copy of "the latest issue of *Architectural Design* (edited by Charles Jencks) with examples of classical post-Modernism included". It is clear from the sketch that the design solution was not proposed purely as a post-Modern idea. Rather it shows how a post-Modern solution might be developed out of the difficulties presented by the site. The solution is clearly proposed on the basis of the context of the site (the word context is underlined in the letter), specifically in providing a formal end to the vista down King Street.

This sketched proposal should be taken more as a thought than a fully worked-out design, but it was the seed from which the final design would grow. It shows, as noted on the sketch, a "long, off-the-peg, simple lean-to greenhouse..., rather demure and hidden" closed at one end by an immense eight-columned Roman triumphal arch, its paired columns (a device much used by Wren) surmounted by a shallow pediment with an oval lunette.

By December 1980 it was clear a proposal on this basis would get the green light, and more detailed work

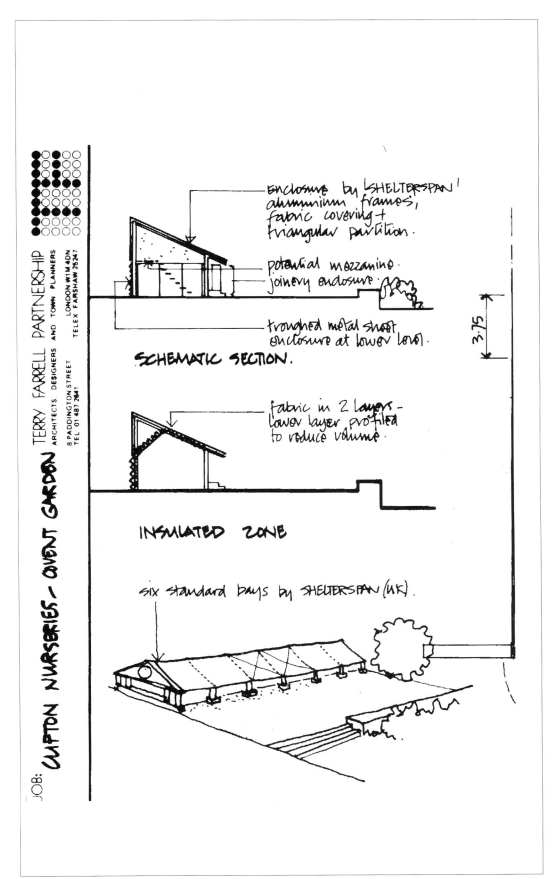

This more developed study proposes a Shelterspan fabric roof in six bays over an aluminium frame. with a mezzanine underneath and troughed metal sheet enclosure on the side wall.

The columns were a major feature of the facade design, and Craig Downie and Terry Farrell mocked up a column in the office (facing, top left) to study the precise profile before adopting the final design (facing, below). They also created a fanciful post-Modern garden column (facing, right) from hose-pipe sections and plant-pots, as the centrepiece of an AD exhibition. The perspective (above) showing the finished building shining out of the gloom of Covent Garden was used as a cover design by AD when the building opened.

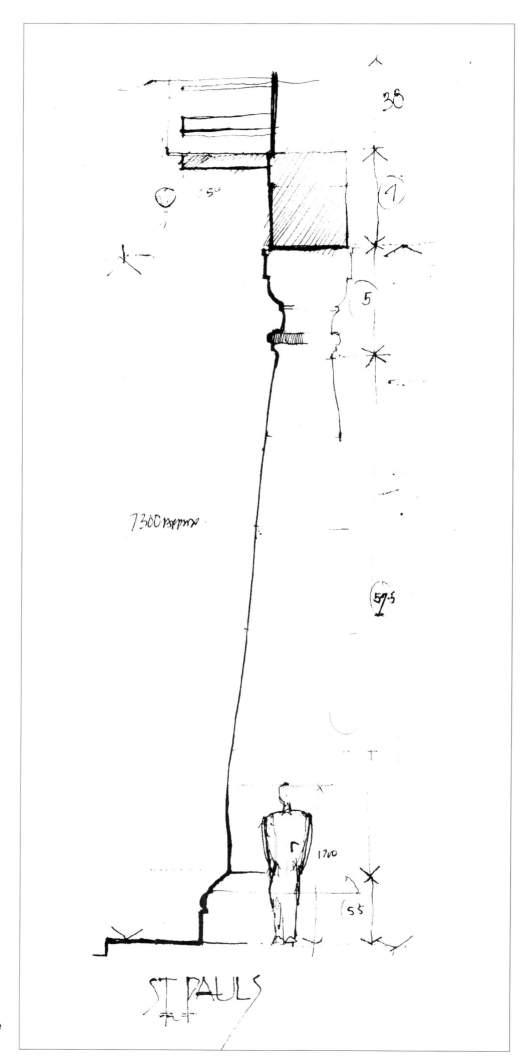

Oliver Richards' sketch for different solutions to the Clifton's facade also includes a scale drawing of the pillars fronting St Paul's Church at the other end of the Piazza.

These two views of St Paul's Church were taken by Craig Downie while researching the garden shop design. The portico surmounted by a lunette was transferred to the shop in several studies for the facade. Farrell particularly liked the fact that the portico on the church was also a false front: the entrance to the church is at the side of the building, just as the entrance to the shop was to be.

began to formulate the shape of the building. A sketch dated December 15th, by Oliver Richards, an architect in Farrell's office who was the first job architect for the Covent Garden building, repeats the colonnaded pediment with a central round window, with six columns down the long side marking the six bays into which the garden shop was to be divided. This is enclosed by a fabric-covered triangular roofspace provided by Shelterspan, with whom Farrell and Partners had been discussing another fabric-roofed temporary building project. This was an invitation to design a temporary trade exhibition space beside the Alexandra Palace in north London, recently gutted by fire. Farrell had noted in his diary in early December that "we are front runners on the Ally Pally", and Oliver Richards moved from the Covent Garden building to take over the post of job architect when the commission came through. He later worked on the TV-AM building for Farrell before setting up in practice on his own.

By Christmas Eve 1980 Farrell was sufficiently clear about the design concept for Covent Garden to write to Philip Tavener, the director of Clifton Nurseries who was to be responsible for the Covent Garden building, that he had "all you need to give the design go-ahead". This was to be for a solution "much more economic than a conventional greenhouse... a very simple, basic 'shed', very ele-

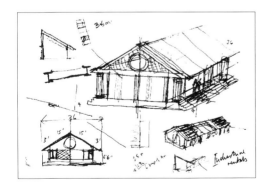
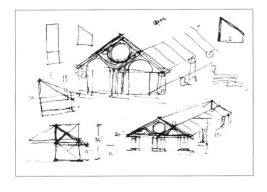

The plan and elevation (right) shows the trompe-l'oeil pediment, and the floor plan and internal layout for the garden shop. The restriction to the edge of the site in Covent Garden did not allow for the free-flowing building proposed to Clifton Nurseries for their Bayswater site (facing, above). The two buildings are compared in the perspective sketch (facing): though different in design both buildings relied on high-technology lightweight engineering, provided by Peter Rice of Ove Arup.

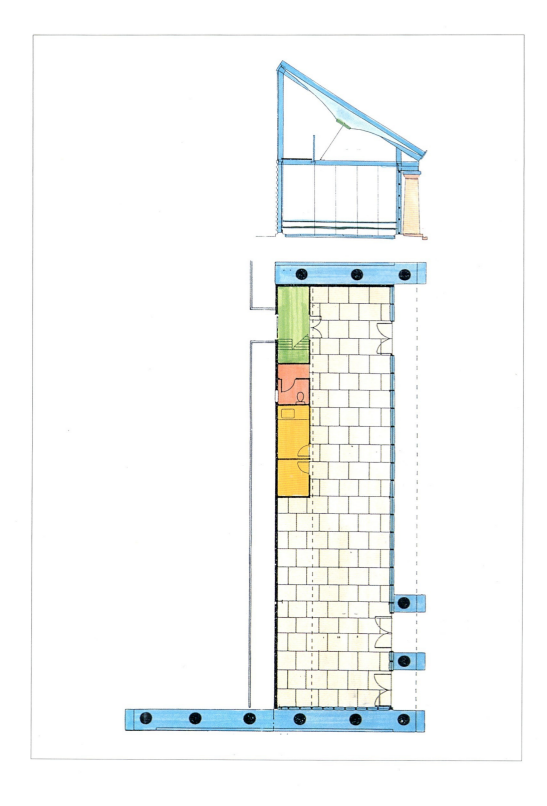

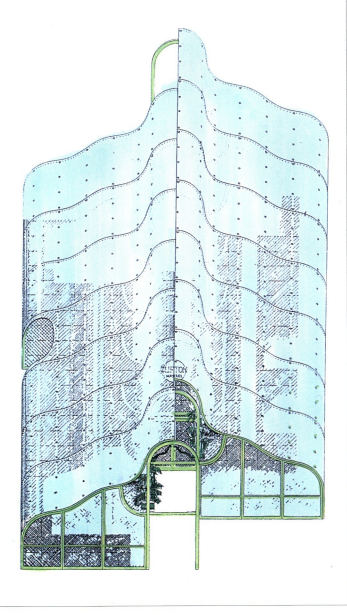

47

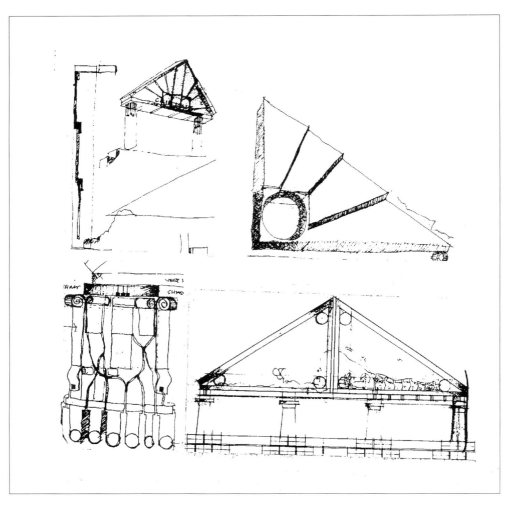

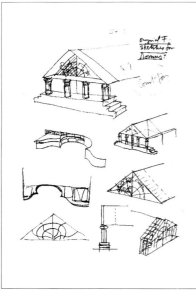 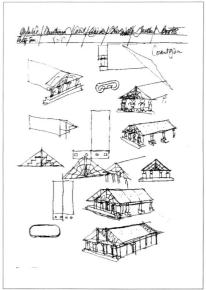

Sketches to establish the design of the facade and the pediment, by Craig Downie (above) and Terry Farrell. Trained as a painter, Farrell used sketches extensively to develop design ideas.

Craig Downie's sketch shows the floral decoration of the facade, with greenery growing through and over the pediment, and openwork columns flanking the entrance.

The colour of the steelwork (above) was a crucial element in the design, and the quality of the work was also critical, as much of the steelwork would be exposed to view (facing, above). The roof (facing, below) was made from a single piece of Teflon-coated glass cloth, and had to be manoeuvred into place before being tensioned.

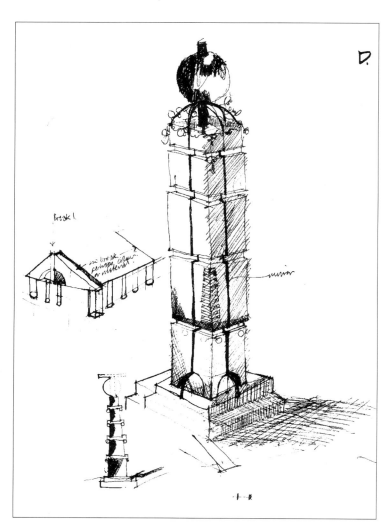

One idea was to echo the design of the garden shop in the adjacent garden, with a free-standing column matching those of the facade: this design is by Craig Downie. But, as the accompanying drawing shows, many different approaches were being researched at once, in outline and in detail, as proposals for a broken pediment jostle with details of fixing the cladding or providing internal shelving.

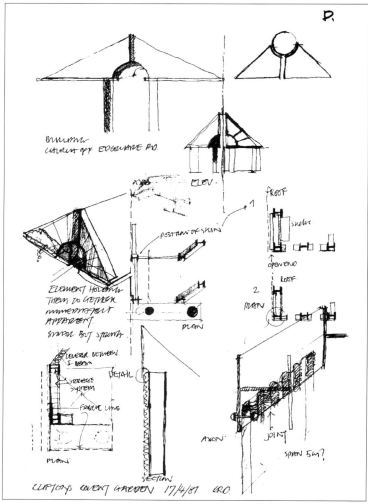

gantly detailed with simple added-on bits of classicism".

To the design of these classical details the architects now turned. Craig Downie, with less than two years' professional experience, had joined recently Farrell & Partners as an assistant architect, and he took over as job architect from Oliver Richards. Craig had applied to work for Farrell because of his interest in technology, and he acknowledges that with Farrell he "learned more about technology than he expected to, and in unexpected ways as well." On the other hand, he admits that when he took over the Covent Garden building he knew scarcely anything about classical architectural detail. "Terry lent me a copy of Bannister Fletcher", Craig recalls, "as at school in Aberdeen I'd concentrated on building systems and planning rather than history."

The design process, in what was still an office of a dozen people, was very direct. Farrell recalls that he would often do rough sketches and drawings for details at home in the evenings: "I quite liked working on the kitchen table with the family all around me: I'd worked that way since I was at school." The drawings would be discussed with the job architect the next morning, either at the drawing board or in meetings. "In meetings I'd tend to draw on anything that came to hand: envelopes, scrap paper, whatever. One client kept one of the drawings on an envelope and framed it, and gave me a Filofax in return. Needless to say at the next meeting I didn't have any paper - I'd given the Filofax to my wife! The client was hugely amused - he'd bet with his partner that I'd do just that."

Farrell's use of drawing to develop design ideas is, he agrees, a result of his interest in painting. "They weren't formal drawings," he says, "but just sketches, often with comments and remarks scribbled in the margins or across the sheet. They were an informal way of developing ideas, which would carry on in discussions and design meetings." Craig Downie remembers that Farrell would regularly appear in the morning with new suggestions and proposals. "He'd never sit down," Craig says, "just stand by the board and show me his ideas, comment on what I was doing, and direct me." In this way they both pursued a variety of solutions to the pediment (broken, open, and pierced with a single window) and to the columns, making a photographic and drawn survey of the surrounding Covent Garden buildings, particularly of the Inigo Jones St Paul's Church at the opposite end of the Piazza. There are drawings for facades with six or eight columns in pairs, for four large single columns, and for the six columns finally adopted. The columns are Doric, then Tuscan, rusticated, then pulvinated. There is even a design for a column surmounted by a sphere, echoed by a three-quarter circle scooped from the top of the pediment.

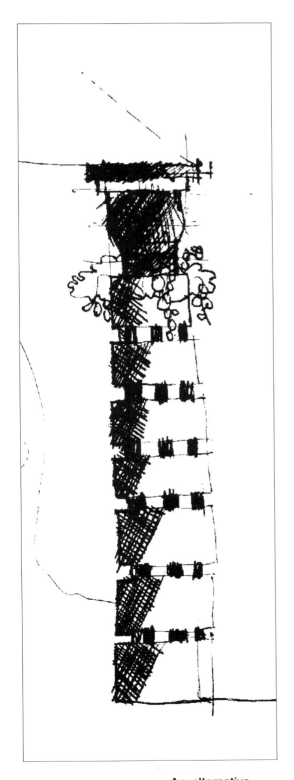

An alternative sketch for the main column, incorporating a series of plant trays to create the shaft.

Terry Farrell and Craig Downie (on left) on site just after the roof had been fixed (left). The buttons used to tension the central area of each roof panel, together with luff grooves at the edges, can be seen merged into the total design (below, left) and as a design feature (below, centre and right). The translucency of the Teflon-coated fabric was valuable in the daytime and spectacular at night (facing).

The exterior of the temple of Athena at Paestum, one of the finest surviving Greek temples.

One design was for an openwork column, in which plants would grow. Another columnar idea was mocked up in the office from lengths of hosepipe and a plant pot, supplied by Clifton Nurseries - it was featured in an *Architectural Design* exhibition on post-Modernism at Leinster Gardens, in London: as Terry recalls, "it was an interesting and quite important by-product of the Clifton Nurseries buildings, being a proper classical column, though not a very academic one!"

The design work for the Clifton Nurseries building took place in a relatively short space of time, in the two to three months from January to March 1981. Few of the surviving drawings are dated, so it is not possible to order a progression of designs. In any event, it is clear from the drawings themselves that all the options - form and number of columns, shape and decoration of pediment, and so on - were all open all the time, until they coalesced into the final design. The design process was largely between Farrell and Craig Downie: though Jacob Rothschild was regularly shown drawings and suggestions his role seems to have been one of encouragement. A letter from Philip Tavener in January 1981, concerning the design for the facade, encourages Farrell to be even bolder: "JR... has something much more flamboyant in mind." As Lord Rothschild recalls, "I thougth that Farrell's type of post-Modernist architecture was full of wit and humour but also had a very serious side." Craig Downie pointed out that the same free-flow approach to design applied elsewhere, even to larger and more complex buildings such as TV-AM: "when I moved on to that after Clifton, we completely changed the arrangement and decoration of the street frontage and the central arch, just as the rest of the building was evolving around us."

From this flurry of activity, according to Craig Downie, a possible outside model emerged, the 5th century Greek temple of Athena at Paestum, north of Naples, one of the best preserved Greek temples, which

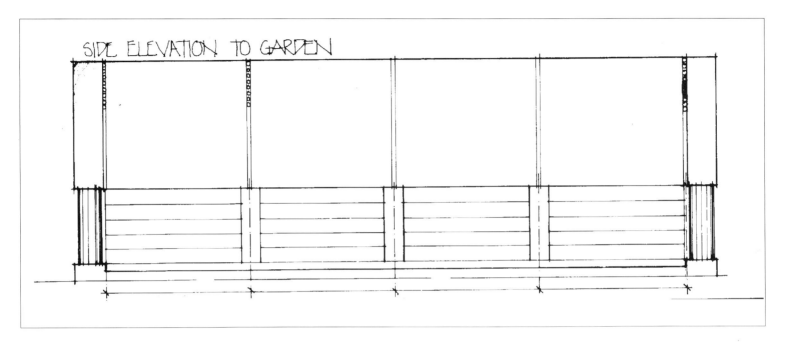

Inigo Jones would probably have seen on his travels in Italy in 1614. This has a plain Doric order of six columns under a clear pediment, with a shallow frieze and pediment fronting the pronaos and longitudinal inner walls of blocked stonework. But in a way this came too late. Clifton Nurseries was never pure Paestum. Craig Downie admits that Paestum was a help, but that the final form really emerged from the surrounding area: "the proportions and in particular the curve of the columns were chosen because of the vistas down King Street, and across the Piazza. We made a cardboard full-size mockup of the column and I remember spending ages trying various degrees of curvature to get it right, both in the office, and on one famous Saturday morning, on site with Terry, marking, measuring and viewing different positions and sizes, under the gaze of some bemused tourists." Craig Downie worked on the design of the columns with Alan Morris, a graduate of the Architectural Association then working in Farrell's office. Morris was also involved in the manufacture of the columns: he went on to design the interior furniture at TV-AM for Farrell.

The final design was not only an aesthetic solution. It also met the needs of the garden shop, by providing

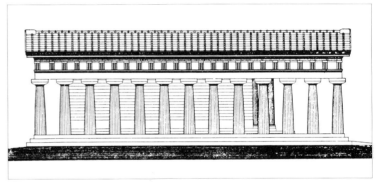

The first proposed elevation to the garden of the Clifton nurseries building (top) used horizontal elements separated by pillars as in the hypothetical reconstruction of Paestum (below). In the final solution glass panels framed in hardwood were used, in a pattern deliberately intended to recall the stone blocks forming the walls of St Paul's Church.

This interior view of the finished building shows how the exposed steelwork and Teflon roof integrated with the display of plants for which the shop was built.

The 20% translucency of the Teflon roof was ideal for dramatic night-time effect.

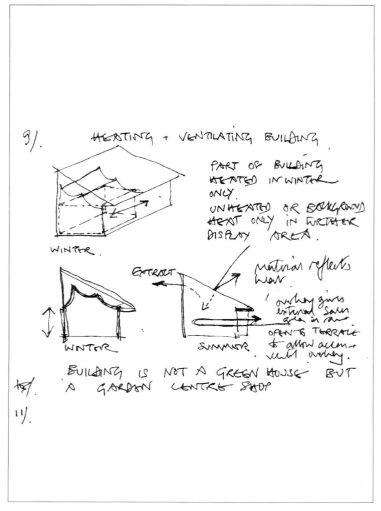

This page from minutes of a client meeting shows Farrell's close involvement with the running and working of the shop, even though the interior fitting was originally Clifton's responsibility. The way in which the roof and mezzanine also contributed to the final effect can be seen in the photograph on the facing page.

potential open and closed areas for displaying different varieties of plant. To this end the side wall was to be opened visually onto the adjoining garden by making the wall of glass, with wooden pine framing replacing the mortared joints, in a rusticated pattern derived from the side walls of temples.

Inigo Jones's St Paul's Church also provided a model, but more than that it was an inspiration. Viewed from the outside, as Farrell points out, it shows a traditional temple layout, with its pillars and arches modified to suit the London context. However, the actual arrangement of the church is contrary to its external appearance. Since the altar had to be at the east end of the building, the entrance under the portico (at the east end of the church and fronting the Piazza) is a false one. "The entrance is at the opposite end of the building, through the churchyard, and arranged according to the different street context at the west end," Farrell continues, "so form does not follow function; rather, form responds to the realities of the situations at the two ends of the building, separated from each other by the intervening buildings of King Street and Henrietta Street. The realization that Inigo Jones had adapted his classical vocabulary to the actual context of his building gave me the feeling that I too was free to adapt my temple to the realities of the new Covent Garden. Jones's handling of the classical model validated my treatment of it: as an example of urban planning St Paul's Church is very complex and very subtle. It gave me both a stimulus, a pretext and a challenge to do as well in a similar task." Today Farrell frankly admits that in 1980 he was not familiar with the classical vocabulary of architecture, "I wasn't trained in classical architecture: I was in unknown territory, in a way, despite the experience of working with Jencks. I wanted to have fun with the building, while being aware that, unlike the Colonnades, the Covent Garden building could not be context-free - shouldn't be context-free - because of its site."

A revised planning application was submitted in February 1981, and the required temporary building licence was issued in April. The notes to a design meeting earlier that month sum up the concerns of the period. At the end of Farrell's notes he wrote in capital letters 'BUILDING IS NOT A GREENHOUSE BUT A GARDEN CENTRE SHOP'. The first note concerns how the building is to be used, interacting with the adjoining garden and not independent from it. (An early plan had the shop adjoining a raised terrace overlooking the garden, but this had been discarded.) Apart from security considerations, the two main areas covered by the notes are the "shop window role" of the entrance portico and the nature of the roof and internal mezzanine (a feature retained from the very first proposal for the L-shaped building) in the working of the whole. For Farrell it was very important that the function of the building as a garden shop should "breathe through the architecture".

This became even more important in the design of the pediment. The right-hand half pediment would be glazed, but not the left, but the decoration of the whole pediment needed to be consistent, and not too encroaching. A variety of designs were sketched, including an angled ziggurat (the steps supporting plant troughs, according to a note on the drawing), a radial sunburst and a pair of semi-circles. One design suggests backing the pediment with strips of coloured fabric, or with mirrors. The final design was for a pair of semicircles with three lines on each side radiating from the base, one complete radius at forty-five degrees, the others, at thirty and sixty degrees, only joining the inner semicircle to the hypotenuse. This arrangement happily echoes another familiar garden object, the face of a sundial. It supplied the necessary support while interfering minimally with the view through the pediment to the plants within or around it. In the final design, the blank, left-hand half of the pediment would be stepped back from the right-hand

The completed design (facing) brought the floral element out of doors with living swags of flowers between the columns. and illuminated lettering on the facade. A decade later (above) the swags are gone and the bin-men and burgers have taken over.

The design of the columns posed two problems: they needed to be integrated into the shop, and make a design statement of their own, Farrell was very keen to make the link with living floral decoration on the columns. Three drawings show this idea being developed, in the capitals of the columns (top left) and in the links between them (top right): the details of the hooks are worked out in a third drawing (bottom left).

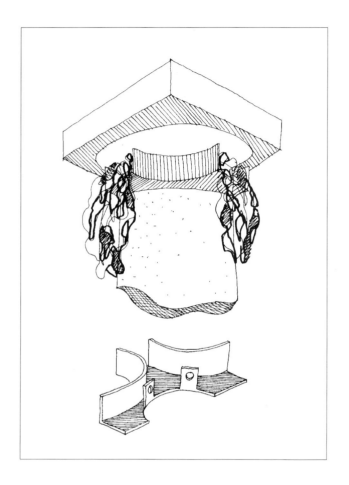

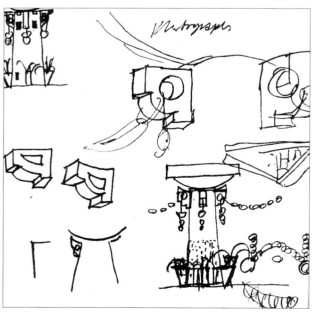

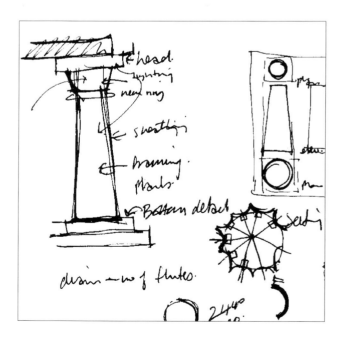

At the same time as looking at the floral decoration, the columns themselves were studied, for example with illuminated capitals (bottom right), or with exaggerated or reversed entasis and fluting (facing page top) and by the use of colour highlights in red and blue on the columns themselves (facing page below).

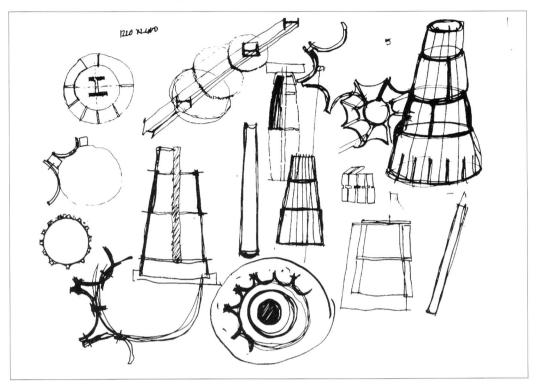

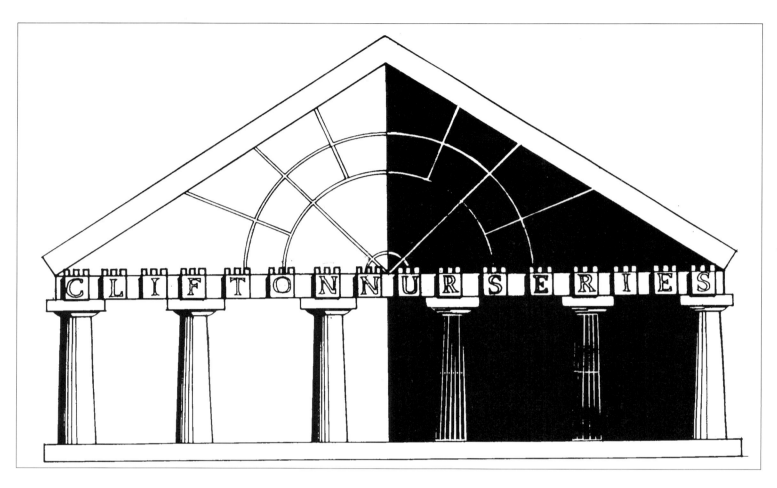

The building as it was presented to the press in December 1981 had unadorned columns, as in the above drawing and photograph.

part. This not only provided a welcome complexity to the facade, but also a ledge on which plants could be displayed, as when Christmas trees were placed there at the shop's opening in December 1981.

From an early stage it had also been Farrell's intention to make several of the columns in open metalwork, so that plants could be grown within them, as they would also grow over the swags linking the columns, so making a "living facade" (at one point, according to Craig Downie, all the columns were to be open ones). The "fake" end of the facade - that half fronting the car park - would be planted out in different seasons, so that the facade would change with the year, and the unadorned architecture be decorated with real floral swags. But the end Clifton Nurseries decided that putting so many plants in the open would invite theft, and the idea had to be dropped. Nevertheless for Farrell the inside/outside nature of the building

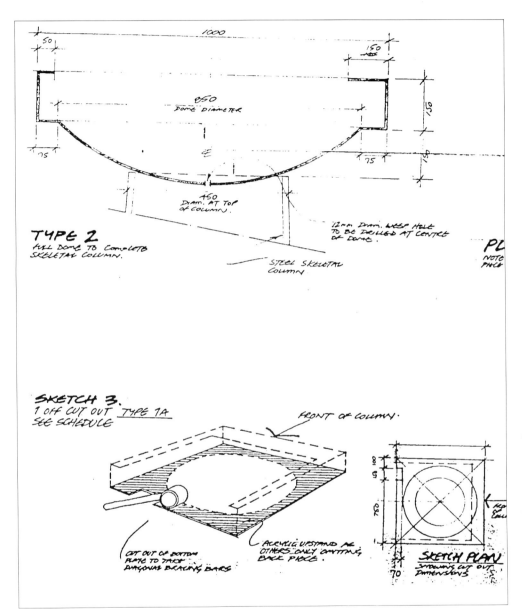

The capitals to the columns, as suggested in an early sketch (below) were to be illuminated, as was the lettering on the frieze. Craig Downie's sketch (left) shown the form of the capitals.

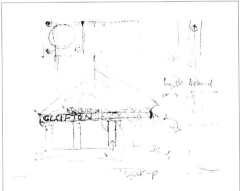

was a key element in its design: some of his earliest notes had emphasized how the appearance of the building would change with the seasons. To leave an empty facade screening a car park was unacceptable to him. The final form of the building therefore incorporated metalwork floral swags hung on Greek key hooks between the left-hand columns, decorative fillets on the left-hand columns and coloured panels on the echinoi. These were designed by Farrell himself with David Goodfellow at Clifton Nurseries, as Craig Downie had by then moved on also to TV-AM. In fact, these final design details were not ready

The final version of the facade had swags of flowers between the left-hand columns, and decorated panels on the echinus of each, as in this drawing and photograph.

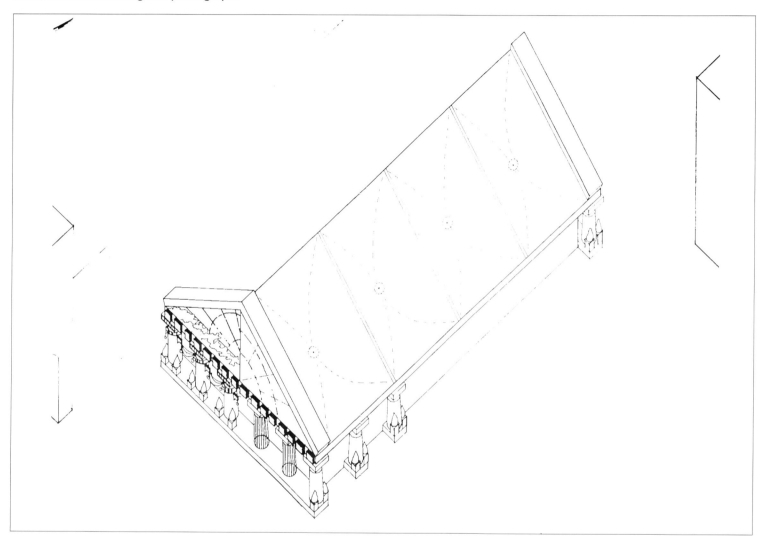

until February 1982, some two months after the building had formally opened, and they were put in place a month later. At the same time, the columns were changed around, two skeletal ones being moved in front of the shop window, to "give better transparency into the shop". Previously one column had been in front and the other on the side. This work was done over a weekend at the end of March, 1982.

At the time there were those who preferred the unadorned front of the building: Charles Jencks, for example, was, according to Farrell "adamant that the first solution was the right one". But these critics did not realize that the floral decorations, especially the swags, had been part of the design from the beginning. The red keylines on the echinus panels provide additional contrast, emphasizing the *trompe-l'oeil* effect by highlighting the difference between the two halves of the facade, while the gold diglyphs carry the eye around the building to the triglyphs under the roofline. This deliberate increase in the visual complexity of the building crowns the design. On April 5th 1982, Terry Farrell was able to write to Philip Tavener and Jacob Rothschild about the "aesthetic decision to make a cameo of the left hand side which is balanced as an entity separate from the 'real' right hand side ... I feel strongly that our final contribution completes the architectural effect and am very conscious that the architectural ambitions of the building are as much our design as Cliftons, as client." Farrell concludes "I am therefore happy to contribute all the work carried out over this weekend (when the final details were put into place) as our contribution to Cliftons and Covent Garden."

Sharing the design credit with the client was not mere modesty: as Farrell says, although Jacob Rothschild never interfered in the design, "it was a very important building for him, and it was my first building in a very public space. There were a lot more Oxbridge types with a knowledge of architectural history about in Covent Garden than there were in Bayswater, and so working on a centre-stage building perhaps made me less experimental and more nervous. We were all, Jacob Rothschild as well, under pressure to make a success of the building. I didn't want to descend the slippery slope into pure classical allusions. I'd got into post-Modernism through being contextual, not because I needed an architectural language. In Covent Garden I was in unknown territory, and I may have reined myself in in consequence. I probably enjoyed doing the first Clifton Nurseries building more than the second, for that reason, and when Maggie Keswick told me that she thought the Covent Garden building was a triumph, I felt very pleased and very relieved."

Some critics, notably Charles Jencks, preferred the plainer version of the facade, but as this photograph shows, the final touches added dramatically to the visual effect of the building.

PUTTING UP A SIGNIFICANT SHED

Craig Downie (back to camera) and Brian Forster of Ove Arup on site.

The plan of the Covent Garden building was based on a grid of four five-metre square bays, taking up the whole width of the site, and side on to the garden Clifton's were creating on the site of the Italian Garden. On this plan a monopitch structure would be built, with continuous solid rear and end walls, the first bay open onto the garden and returning under the colonnade, to form the shop entrance, which opened onto the garden. The three remaining bays were to be enclosed with glass and timber on the garden side. Farrell had tried to ascertain what the below-ground conditions were - no-one seemed quite to know, and one theory was that a hotel had previously stood on the site, so the new building would be over its basements, presumably since filled-in; therefore low ground loadings were needed. Because of this uncertainty, and because a steel frame could be erected quickly and economically, and easily dismantled once the site was reclaimed by the Opera House, a steel frame was the appropriate solution. Most importantly, this form of construction gave maximum play to the design possibilities of a building intended to fit into the relaxed atmosphere of the revived Covent Garden, with its mixture of shops, cafes and public leisure spaces. The design had to respect its architectural context, but it did so, in the words of

The pediment being hoisted into position: erecting the steel frame only took a single day.

architect's draft press release, "with an occasional ironic, but knowing, irreverence". For Farrell, both then and subsequently, it has been important for his buildings "to make a deliberate reference to alternative building forms, through a collage approach, and through an awareness of

Four views of the site with foundations being poured: uncertainties about the conditions below grounds were to increase the costs.

scale and context... Rather than being a statement of the architect's style, a building needs to be a relevant object for its site. It was easier for me to make a temple-object at Covent Garden, precisely because I wasn't familiar with the classical language then."

If among the temple sources were Inigo Jones' Tuscan St Paul's Church, and the Temple at Paestum, there is one considerable difference between the models and the final building. This is partly the considerable reduction in height of the frieze, but more importantly in the pitch of the pediment, which is much steeper than any Greek original. There are three main reasons for this. The first is practical, in that with such a long but narrow building any gain in interior height added to the available space, and in this particular case Clifton Nurseries needed a high roofspace both for climate control and to display mature indoor plants to advantage - the choice of an open mesh floor for the mezzanine was also made partly as a result of these considerations.

The second reason for the steep pitch of the roof was to do with the site. The building, as we have seen, needed to close the vista down King Street and balance the surrounding architecture, and to do so it needed to gain height. But the third reason was dictated by the nature of the roof itself.

The original intention behind the garden buildings projects was to put together low-cost temporary structures, and in the case of the Colonnades building this had been achieved by a novel use of a double-skinned polycarbonate cladding around a standard steel frame. At the same time that Covent Garden was being designed, work was in progress on the Alexandra Palace pavilion, another high-tech temporary structure. Terry Farrell was into lightweight structures, and was already working closely with Peter Rice and Brian Forster of the engineering company Ove Arup, where Peter Rice headed the Lightweight Structures division. For this reason it seemed logical that the project must have an unusual and innovative solution on the engineering level as well as the aesthetic one. "I'd inherited an interest in lightweight structures from the Farrell Grimshaw days," Farrell recalls, "and it seemed the appropriate vocabulary to use when these projects came up; after all, in the Alexandra Palace project it was a condition that the building be taken down at the end of the lease, and the Colonnades building was also sold and re-erected when the site was redeveloped."

Work on the site began in April 1981. The first thing to do was remove the existing garden and lay foundations for the new garden and the garden shop. Victor Shanley of Clifton Nurseries, who designed the new garden, recalls that "the plant troughs from the old garden were put into store at our depot, and looked

The temporary pavilion for Alexandra Palace designed by Farrell, with a fabric roof engineered by Peter Rice of Ove Arup.

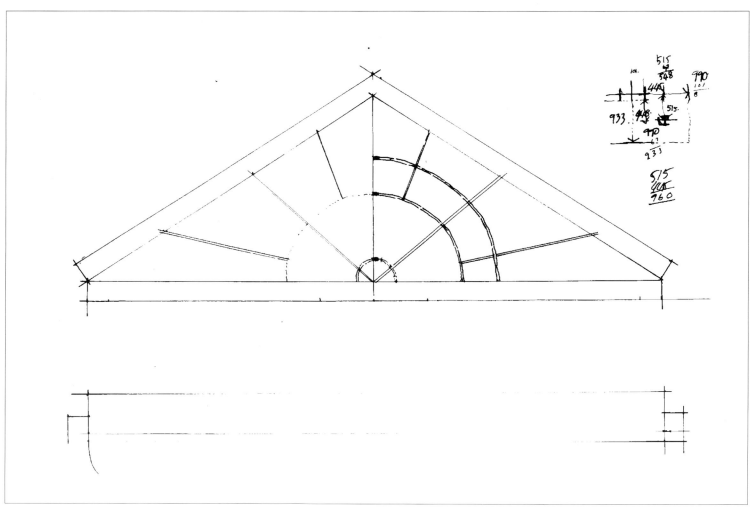

Final drawings for the steelwork of the rear pediment.

after until the people from the Forum wanted them." Breaking up the old basements was not so easy, and unexpected costs and delays occurred, both on the garden site and the shop. Even plumbing the single staff toilet into the mains was a nightmare, Craig Downie recalls. "No-one had realized how deep the sewers were, and eventually ex-miners had to dig out a shaft, adding nearly four thousand pounds of unexpected costs." To reduce costs on the job, a quantity surveyor was not engaged, nor were full working drawings made up in advance. Wiltshiers, who were the project managers on TV-AM, were asked to provide project management only on a cost-saving basis, and indeed their site foreman was shared with another job. "I think it was the only time I've written out a formal Architects Instruction for someone to buy a bag of screws," Craig Downie recalls. "I forcibly learned a great deal about project management because of the need to save costs." Craig also benefited from working with Ove Arup, who were appointed consulting engineers. In all the total cost of the building was just over 100,000 pounds, including fitting out the interior and other additional services. For a building constructed to such a high specification, and for which all services had to be brought onto the site, the cost was not excessive, though higher than standard retail shell buildings of the time. And there was always the intention of dismantling the building at the end of the lease, to re-use it or sell it on.

While the foundations were being laid, Craig Downie and the team at Ove Arup set down to the detailed design of the steelwork, which was supplied by Knight and Butler Ltd. They submitted the lowest tender of the six sought by Craig Downie, coming in at 9,250 pounds, under half the highest bid. The whole frame was to be in standard 203 by 133 universal steel sections, to save costs. "Knight and Butler did very well," Brian Forster recalls, and Craig Downie pointed out that tolerances on the finished job were very high. Thus in the final building the setting-out error was limited to about two millimetres in the whole twenty-metre length of the building. "It was like a building by Mies van der Rohe," Craig recalls, "the fit of parts was so exact."

This level of quality control was achieved by test-erecting the steelwork elements at Knight and Butler's factory in Lingfield before its delivery to the site. There were three individual monopitch sections, which once in place on the grid were connected horizontally by 203 by 133 universal beams to form the rigid frame. The three half pediments were each constructed in advance as single units, and once the two units for the front pediment were sleeved together on site, the pediments were craned into position and the raked roof beams attached to them.

The pediment once completed in sections was erected at Knight and Butler's factory to check the fit: these photos show the test erection in progress.

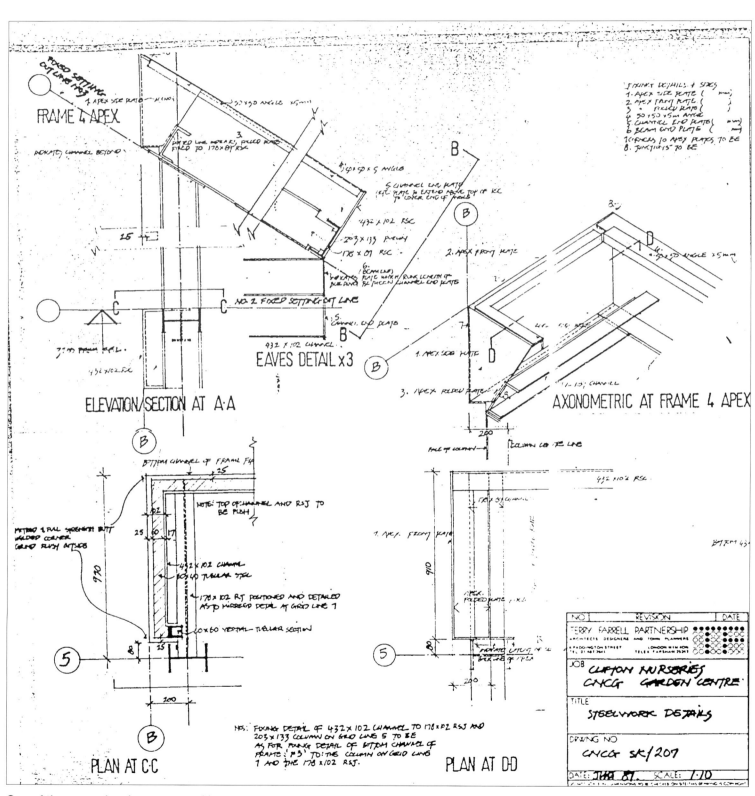

One of the many drawings prepared by Craig Downie for the steelwork details.

"Like something by Mies": The steelwork being erected and fitted into place.

Craig's attention to detail paid off in the steelwork, not only in the roof but also in the pediment, where the glazed panels had to be fitted. "It proved impossible to make the glass in a single piece. Preedy's, who supplied the glass, pointed out that the lower right hand angle would have inevitably broken under its own weight if made in a single piece." In the end the glass was made up of four vertical panels to follow the hypotenuse of the pediment. The frame of the pediment alone supports the glass, with no glazing sub-frame, partly because Farrell was concerned to keep transparency as high as possible, and any additional vertical supports for the glass panels would have vitiated this. It was also important that the glazed corner of the pediment, where the left-hand half was set back from the right-hand half, should be in effect invisible.

The erection of the steel frame was achieved in a single day, though the building was not plumbed into line and the bolts fully tightened until the roof was in place. The steel framework was painted in a deep blue colour, selected by Farrell and Craig Downie, although the pediment was painted Sherwood green. "I was very pleased with the blue colour and the effect of the painted steelwork was very striking," says Craig, "but one day I found myself confronted on site by Lord Drogheda, one of the trustees of the Opera House, and a director of Clifton Nurseries, who was most worried: he was surprised that the building looked so big and was it all going to be the same colour? However, I was able to reassure him that the building was to the size on the plans, and would have a white roof."

The steel frame was selected because of its relatively low weight, and the same considerations applied to the roof. A Pvc roof membrane had been considered early on, since the translucency of the roof was a key element in designing a greenhouse building. In May 1981 Terry Farrell noted in his diary "call Peter Rice at Arup's about the roof question". A further note in the diary, for the

21st of May, highlighted a potential solution. Clearly scribbled during a phone conversation, the note reads "Brian says DS class is 476 and he said met by Teflon and not by Pvc." Teflon is a polytetrafluoroethelyne, discovered by the Dupont company in the USA in 1943 and developed as an industrial laminate, most familiarly in its application as a non-stick coating for cookware. Applied as a coating to woven glass cloth, however, it has excellent protective properties, and is flame-resistant, as the District Surveyor's test category, cited by Brian Forster on the phone to Farrell, had shown. It also had twenty percent translucency. Fothergill and Harvey Structures, in Derby, the British agents for Dupont, had already seen the material used for altar canopies during the Pope's visit to Ireland in 1979, and were eager to find a showcase building for the material in England. This opportunity now occurred, but at a cost. Although, according to Brian Forster, the cost differential between Pvc and Teflon-coated glass cloth was four to one, Fothergill and Harvey agreed to supply a Teflon roof for the Covent Garden building at a substantial reduction, in return for an opportunity to use the opening of the building as an occasion to present the material to the technical and architectural press. Ian Dickinson, the then managing director of Fothergill and Harvey Structures, points out that he and his colleagues, particularly Per Bissaert at Dupont in Geneva, had been trying for five years to interest architects and property developers in the new material. "It was, I think, too pioneering," Dickinson says, "and simply ahead of its time. There were a few, like Peter Rice and Terry Farrell, who saw its potential, and now, twelve years later, Teflon is in use increasingly, especially in Europe. But at the time we just couldn't interest people: there wasn't enough discretionary money around in the property business, even then, to try it out. We gave up in the end, not because of cost, but because we got fed up with always knocking on doors and being refused."

Farrell's diary page for 21 May 1981: a scribbled note of a talk with Peter Rice introduces the idea of a Teflon roof.

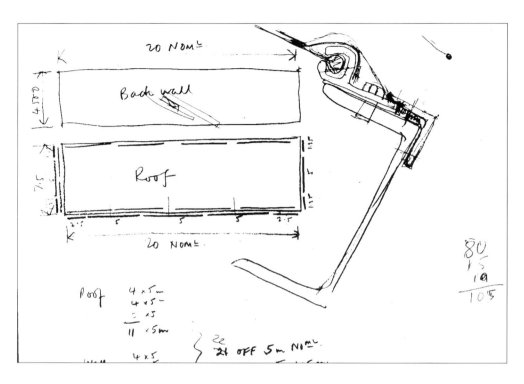

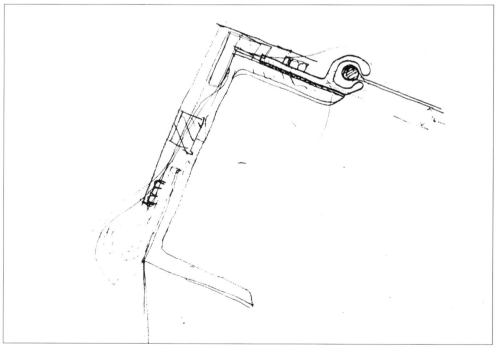

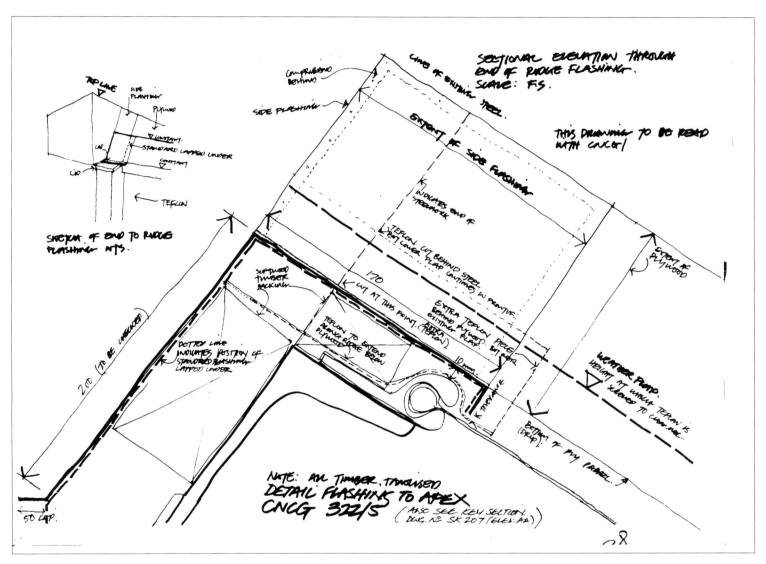

Two rough sketches by Peter Rice (facing page) for the innovative luff groove to hold and tension the Teflon-coated roof. The idea is borrowed from racing yacht technology, where the edge of a sail is secured round a bolt rope, as here, and let into a luff groove to secure the sail to the boom or mast. In the third drawing (above) Craig Downie has worked up the details, both in plan and perspective.

The luff groove secured and tensioned the outer edges of the Teflon-coated glass cloth, and a system of central buttons secured by stays attached to the internal steelwork of the mezzanine were needed to tension the centres. After experimenting with a model (facing page, below) the system was adopted and provided an added visual dimension both internally and externally.

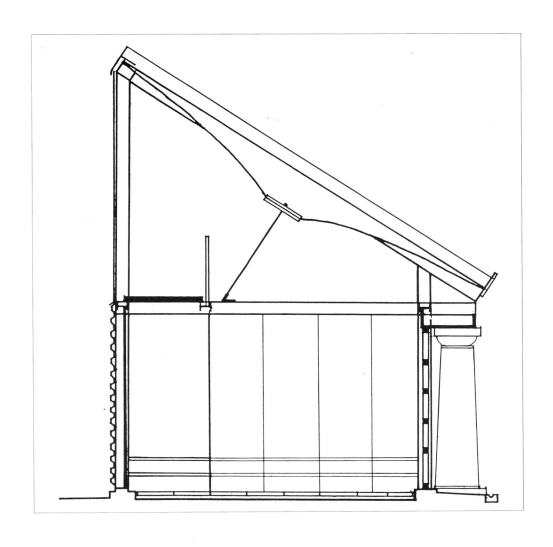

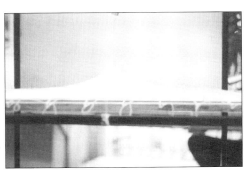

Teflon coated glass cloth is a woven material, and has to be used under tension to maintain its rigidity. Such membrane structures need to be patterned into doubly-curved shapes to assist the tensioning process. Once the material had been adopted, Peter Rice set to work to find the best method of adapting it to the requirements of the building, using a computer to analyze possible designs. It soon became clear that the optimum solution was to make the roof in a single piece, rather than expensively fitting individual sheets to the roof panels. The material could be gripped and tensioned along the main outer edges. This left two design aspects: how to most elegantly fix the edges into the steel roof frame, and how to take up the area of slack in the center of each roof panel, since in each area of fabric there would be a natural "dead" area that could not be tensioned from the perimeter. Craig Downie worked closely with Peter Rice, the consulting engineer, on the solution to this problem.

On the question of fixing the edges of the Teflon-coated glass fibre, an answer was borrowed from yacht technology, where similar problems are encountered fixing the edges of sails to masts and booms. At the edges of the sheet of fabric, the material would be wrapped around a bolt rope, and the rope sandwiched into a luff groove in the metal frame and bolted into place. Using both ends of the building frame as strongbacks, the necessary tension could then be applied, gradually stretching the membrane longitudinally, which had the effect of developing the necessary tension both longitudinally and horizontally. This left the unstressed centres, and here there were two possibilities. Either the centres could be pushed outwards into tension, rather in the way the secondary poles support a circus tent, or they could be pulled inwards to achieve the same result. Clearly the latter solution was preferable aesthetically - otherwise the pushed-out centres would appear above the edge of the pediment and so break up its visual line, but it was also the neatest engineering solution, as

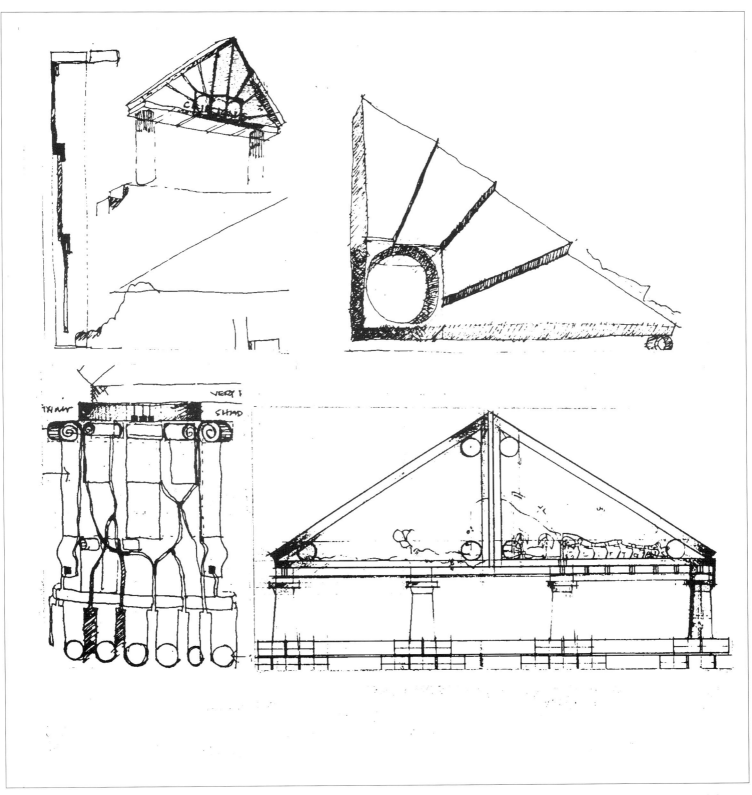

A drawing by Craig Downie for the eaves of the cross members dividing the roof into bays. Even here an alternative is suggested so that the exposed steelwork can be used as a display area.

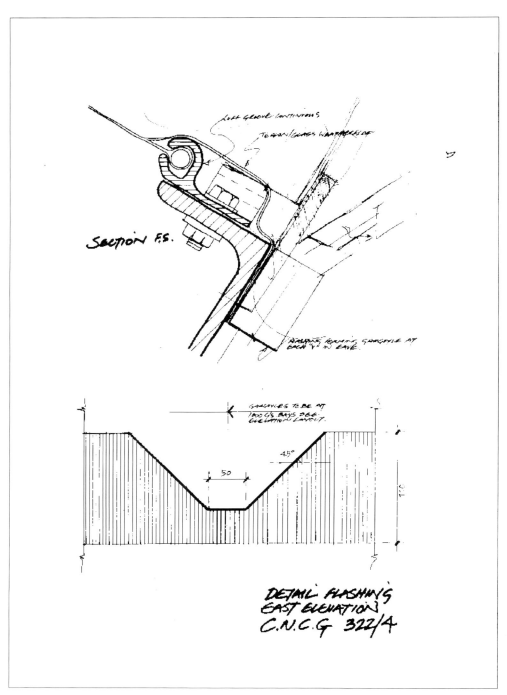

This drawing shows how a weatherflap was provided to cover the luff groove as well as spouts to carry the water away from the side of the building.

the stays holding the centres in tension could then be attached to the mezzanine floor. It was also, according to Brian Forster, more economical.

Once a model had been built to test the roof's appearance and performance, this was the solution adopted, each roof panel being held in its centre by a pair of circular plywood plates or "buttons", each fifity centimentres in diameter, with the fabric sandwiched between them and secured by eighteen bolts. At the centre of the inner plate a ring held the stays, which descended on each side to the outer edge of the mezzanine floor. The shape of the Teflon sheet was determined by patterns calculated by Arups in association with Fothergill and Harvey Structures. Ian Dickinson recalls: "we fabricated the final sheet from Arup's cutting patterns, having developed ourselves the necessary forming machinery." The final configuration was a single sheet composed of four smaller elements, sewn and welded together. The drawings for this, and most of the other engineering elements, were prepared by Alistair Day, Peter Rice and Brian Forster. The bolt ropes, made of nylon and a hefty 30 mm in diameter, could also be used to increase tension as the roof membrane was put into place. When this was done, the edges of the luff groove were bolted home. Along the lower edge of the sheet, above the bolt rope, a continuous flap had been welded, to lap over the luff groove and so provide a waterproof seal. As the building had no guttering on the eaves, Craig Downie had provided spouts to carry rainwater away from the walls below. This solution was by no means perfect and had already worried the client, as the entrance to the shop was under the roof. In July 1981, for example, Philip Tavener wrote to Terry Farrell about guttering: "The thought of one of Mr Rothschild's rich friends walking into the shop through sheet of water appalls me. It worries me even more that an ordinary member of the public may have to do so." Even so, no gutters or downpipes were added.

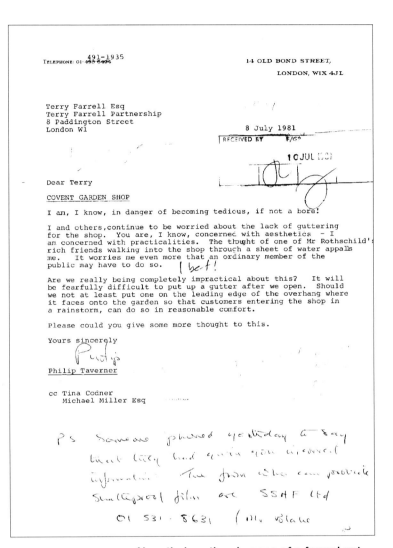

Nonetheless the absence of a formal gutter worried Philip Tavener: Mr Rothschild's friends, let alone members of the public, would risk walking into the shop through a sheet of water. "I bet!" was Farrell's scribbled comment.

With the roof in position, work could start on the end pediment and side wall: the scaffolding seen in these two photos had been retained while putting the roof in place and tensioning it.

The roof was delivered to the site as a single roll of material, and getting it into place caused some problems: "It was not a very manoeuvrable object", is Brian Forster's dry recollection, "and in the end temporary scaffolding had to be put up along the side wall, and the Teflon manhandled into place from there." Craig Downie agrees: "it took quite a bit of manpower and effort to howk it into place." Teflon was also used for the end wall opposite the *trompe-l'oeil* pediment, and for the upper part of the rear wall, above mezzanine level. These smaller sheets were again secured by bolt ropes and luff grooves, and additional tension was supplied by cross-stays mounted on the steelwork frame. In line with the building's unique combination of technology with classical detail, these braces, and the roof stays, were left exposed.

One other problem that had to be provided for was ventilation, as the roof formed a complete and impermeable seal. Like the Colonnades building, which incorporated an ingenious "heat chimney" into the design, the Covent Garden building needed passive ventilation only, using vents in the rear and back wall panels. These were covered with flaps that would open automatically to let hot air escape, but no automation or forced system was necessary. To have such flaps made to order would be have been costly and, even worse, have involved delay, but Craig Downie realized that standard Vent Axia gravity flaps, without their fans and motors, would meet the requirement perfectly. "I had a terrible time persuading Vent Axia to sell me the housings only, without the fans," he recalls, "I think they thought I was mad. But one of the best things I had learnt with Terry Farrell was to look at any material or hardware for what it could do, not just in terms of the manufacturer's intentions."

With the roof in place, work could begin on fitting out the interior. The blue colour of the steelwork, visible

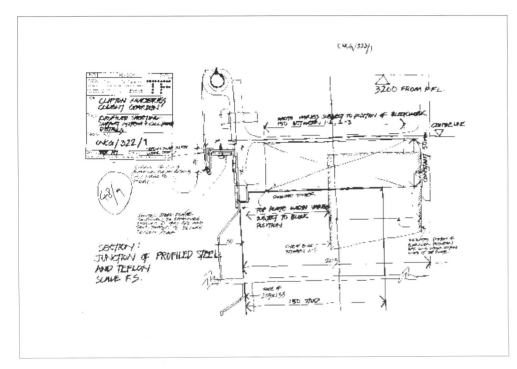

The rear wall, opposite the garden, had a Teflon upper section and profiled steel cladding below the mezzanine level. These two drawings study the joints and cill details. The bracing for the Teflon (centre photo) was deliberately left exposed.

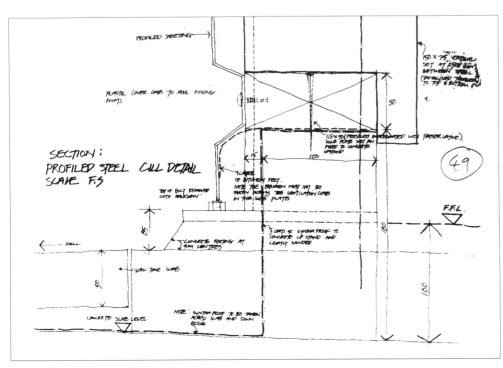

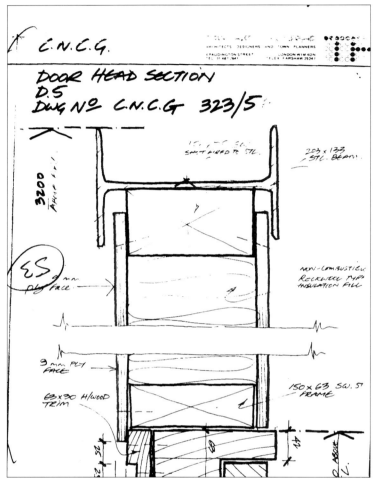
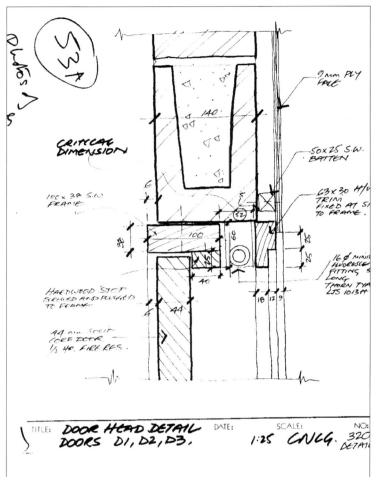

The interior details were equally important: these two drawings show shadow joints (top left) where the plywood met exposed steel girders, and the recessed light fittings over the office doors (below).

in the interior where the steelwork was exposed, was echoed in the fittings. The opaque interior walls were in Polish plywood painted in grey Sadolin with gloss red dado lines, with doors in naturally stained British Columbian pine, the same wood being used to frame the glass panels in the rear three bays facing the garden. "We wanted to give the interior as strong a feeling as the exterior," Craig recalls, "and so a lot of work went into details. For example, joining wood to steel beams is always difficult, because the burr in the steel precludes an exact fit, so I deliberately designed shadow joints, in which the plywood was set back from the steel flange, making a shadow to conceal the actual rather uneven join. The positioning and framing of the internal doors was also a great concern, and I designed hidden lightfittings over each door to highlight them."

In the fourth bay at the front an aluminium-framed entrance space was inserted, running back under the nine columns fronting the pediment and the first bay, again taking up the temple theme by echoing a traditional plan of pronaos and cella. The entrance to the shop was not under the pediment, however, but from the garden side. This emphasized the link between shop and garden, and also echoed the unconventional arrangement of Inigo Jones' church, mentioned above. Of the nine columns, seven were in plywood, painted stone colour, and two in openwork metal, so that climbing plants could grow up and through them, an effect repeated in the interior on the balustrade of the mezzanine floor. The wooden columns, whose function was decorative rather than structural, were assembled by students from the Architectural Association, organized by Stephen Peagu, with the help of Alan Morris. The capitals were made from cream-tinted perspex, so that they could be illuminated at night: Alan Morris found "someone under a railway arch" who worked on props for the film industry to do the perspex forming.

Along the frieze of the facade the words Clifton Nurseries were picked out in illuminated lettering.

The translucency of the Teflon roof increased the daylight effect into the interior, while at night the effect was dramatic.

The interior shop fittings and shelving were designed by Craig Downie with Clifton Nurseries staff, and the interior lighting was also jointly planned. During the daytime the natural light through the glass walling and the white roof was supplemented by Concord uplighters washing onto the Teflon walls, and spotlights to highlight individual areas. At night, however, the effects were more spectacular: the Teflon roof acted as a diffuser for the interior lighting, with the buttons and stays in clear relief, supplemented by floodlamps at the centre base of the main pediment illuminating the Piazza, and down the garden side to light the garden. On the front of the building the illuminated sign picked out the name in softer colours, echoing the greenery visible within. This sign spelt out CLIFTON NURSERIES, running along the frieze of the pediment with each letter in an individual lightbox. Terry Farrell was able to write to Jacob Rothschild in August 1981 that this revision to the design "although large,...is all part of the classical architectural imagery."

THE DRUNKS AND PIGEONS SAW TO THAT...

The building opened on December 1st, 1981, with a press showing at lunchtime and an evening reception, attended by a fashionable crowd including David Frost, for whom Farrell was working at TV-AM. Jacob Rothschild and some of his colleagues had been to Italy on a buying trip, and in addition to plants and shrubs the shop was displaying rattan furniture, antique garden statuary, and maiolica jardinieres. This up-market and original stock complemented the spirit of the newly-reopened market hall across the Piazza, where the Greater London Council, by its rents policy, had deliberately encouraged a mixture of different shopping and eating facilities. Several magazines and newspapers welcomed the new shop as part of the Covent Garden revival: Alastair Best joked about "the second noblest barn in England" and Stephen Gardiner referred to the architect's "flippancy". Lord Rothschild recalls that he was "delighted with the results".

Michael Miller of Clifton Nurseries recalls that the shop had a difficult time living up to its ambitions. This was partly because the shopping profile of Covent Garden was so uneven: there would be office workers looking for plants for desks or window-boxes in the day, and opera-goers looking for orchids in the evening. "We tried

Press comment hailed the new building as a major contribution to the new Covent Garden.

A possible future ... an undated drawing shows the building as a restaurant, with a Teflon roofed-extension to the right. The reality was rather less grand.

a number of marketing strategies, and mixes of merchandise, with several different managers - it was also difficult then to recruit good staff for a short-term site (as we were thinking the two nurseries would be). In fact, the Colonnades did very well over its whole tenure, and Covent Garden broke even."

A report by a security specialist before the building was completed had taken a more jaundiced view of the people of Covent Garden. "The area is rife with vandalism", he wrote, "It is frequented by a very large number of tramp/vagrant types. Most are offensive. Some regularly cause damage when drunk." Describing the greenhouse as an irresistible target, he continues "Fencing would provide little protection unless the specification approached that relating to prisons." He recommends shatter proof film and at least two security guards. In fact the number of glass-breaking incidents was low, although the attentions of drunks and pigeons led to the rapid closing of the sculpture exhibition in the Jubilee Garden adjoining the building, and wandering drunks occasionally bothered staff and customers. Michael Miller points out that the long narrow building was not an ideal retailing space, as with too many customers in it staff found it difficult to move around and help with requests. "Somehow the shop could be either too full or too empty, and it didn't help when the Greater London Council organized large public events in the Piazza. The first time that happened the press of people ruined the planting in the opposite corner of the garden, and we had to start over." Victor Shanley, the garden's designer, agrees. "Because of the focal position of the garden, it was difficult to plan anything but a green thoroughfare. And maintaining the garden was not helped by the homeless people who would sleep there overnight."

With the expiry of the initial lease, uncertainty set in. The Opera House were still intending to redevelop the

The shabby state of the building at present reflects the soured aspirations of the Eighties.

site, now for an office building and backstage space, rather than for the planned second auditorium, and a new extended lease was not on offer, while the rents for a licence were increased. (With the abolition of the Greater London Council the enlightened rents policy in the rest of Covent Garden also gave way to market forces, with ensuing changes in the quality of shopping on offer in the Piazza.) "We didn't feel we could continue in that uncertain situation", Michael Miller comments, "and as we were concentrating our resources at the main nursery in Clifton Villas we had to let the shop go." The building now houses a burger bar: the interior has been radically, not to say brutally, transformed, and the frontage is decaying: parts of the detailing are missing, the capitals are cracked and crooked. Moss and rubbish are filling the buttons in the roof. It's a sad sight.

Lord Rothschild still owns Clifton Nurseries, with Michael Miller as his managing director. Victor Shanley retired from Clifton Nurseries after 37 years there, and is now a garden designer and teacher. Philip Tavener is project director for the new Museum of Commonwealth and Empire in Bristol. Craig Downie, after working for Norman Foster, now has an independent practice as an architect. Alan Morris worked for Eva Jiricna, and is now working in Bologna. Brian Forster still works for Ove Arup, but, sadly, Peter Rice died after a long illness while this book was being prepared. Terry Farrell's practice has continued to grow, with the TV AM building, and developments at London Wall, Vauxhall Cross and Charing Cross among his best known works. He continues as an independent figure, not subscribing either to Modernism or post-Modernism. "I still use a collage approach to my buildings, and seek for an appropriate object as a source, as in the Chinese bowl form I'm using on the Peak building in Hong Kong", he says, "and the lessons I have learnt from smaller buildings move up into the larger projects we are now doing. The Clifton Nurseries building at Covent Garden was an opportunity to work with a discerning client in an architecturally charged and very visible space, an opportunity that doesn't occur too often for an architect. But the idea of the building, with its tensioned fabric roof and architecturally aware details, shows through in current work, for example in another small-scale project, a quayside pub and restaurant in Newcastle upon Tyne, and in the floating canopy for the Edinburgh conference centre. Some architects seem to offer buildings made up of parts off a supermarket shelf, while I try and create a complete meal. I still like the completeness of the Cliftons buildings."